THE MAYO CLINIC DIET

PROTOCOL

Achieve Full Body Transformation and Lose
Weight With Over 120 Delicious Mayo Clinic Diet
Recipes

Zara Anderson M.D.

COPYRIGHT PAGE

PLEASE READ

The ideas, procedures, and recommendations presented in this book are the authors' own. They made them with the best knowledge they had and double-checked them as thoroughly as they could. However, they should not be used in place of professional, one-on-one medical guidance. What each reader does or does not do is entirely up to them. The author and publisher disclaim all responsibility for any harm caused by relying on the information presented here.

TABLE OF CONTENTS

ı

INTRODUCTION

The Mayo Clinic Diet is about restructuring any questionable eating habits and doubling down on healthy staples in the fruit, vegetable, and whole-grain categories — alongside supercharged cuts of protein, and the occasional sweet treat.

By asking you to eat more veggies, fruits, and grains rich in fiber and other nutrients, the Mayo Clinic Diet promises immediate results in the first two weeks of the program: Anywhere between 5 and 10 pounds of weight lost

But the diet's true allure, per experts, could be its design beyond this two-week period, in a phase that promotes two-pounds-per-week weight loss until you've hit your goal in mind. Technically, the Mayo Clinic Diet could be continued for however long you like — and some dieters may stick to its tips and suggestions for the rest of their life.

While the diet doesn't ask you to cut out bread entirely or avoid desserts forever, it does require you to skimp on calories — as few as 1,200 for women and 1,400 for men for the first two weeks.

Understanding Mayo Clinic Diet

If you're like many people who want to lose weight, you've probably tried a number of weight loss programs that didn't work or left you feeling unsatisfied. That's where the Mayo Clinic Diet comes in.

This diet is designed to help you lose weight in a safe and healthy way, without leaving you feeling hungry or deprived.

In this book, we'll explore how and why the Mayo Clinic Diet works, and how it can help you achieve your health and wellness goals. Fortunately, you can learn more about the Mayo Clinic Diet with this master diet guide and cookbook.

Newcomers to the Mayo Clinic Diet will find plenty of guidelines, diet tips, and healthy recipes at their fingertips.

Unlike many other diets that promise quick and drastic weight loss, the Mayo Clinic Diet is designed to help you lose weight gradually and sustainably. The program focuses on making healthy, long-term lifestyle changes rather than simply restricting your calorie intake.

Furthermore, the Mayo Clinic Diet emphasizes the importance of eating a balanced diet that includes plenty of fruits, vegetables, lean proteins, and whole grains. It also encourages regular exercise as a key component of a healthy lifestyle.

History of The Mayo Clinic Diet

Before jumping into any diet, it's wise to learn a little bit about its origins. Some diets are built upon solid research and study, and some are faddish, get-rich-quick plans that are often unhealthy and make promises they can't possibly deliver.

When it comes to the Mayo Clinic Diet, the name behind the diet belongs to one of the most respected medical organizations in the world, so it's no surprise the diet is popular.

The world's first integrated, group private practice, the Mayo Clinic brings doctors, researchers and medical experts together for the purpose of education, research and treatment. Today, the Mayo Clinic boasts around 55,000 health care professionals, and comprises three clinics and four hospitals

In addition to its research and educational initiatives, the Mayo Clinic has helped treat more than 6 million people since its founding in 1863.

With the organization's impressive history and reputation, it's no wonder that people are interested in the Mayo Clinic Diet, which doesn't involve counting calories or cutting out carbohydrates.

Philosophy of The Mayo Clinic Diet

The Mayo Clinic Diet focuses on building new healthy habits and breaking old, less healthy habits — think of it as a "lifestyle approach."

The diet has two main principles, which includes:

- Follow an eating plan that's low in calories but includes foods that fill you up and that you enjoy eating

- Using physical activity to burn more calories

The Mayo Clinic Diet eating plan is low in fat and calories and prioritizes whole grains, fruits and vegetables.

The diet also has two phases lasting 12 weeks, with the option to continue for as long as you would like the support. Your program is customizable, as well. You can choose meal plans that are keto-friendly, high in protein, vegetarian or Mediterranean.

PART I: The Mayo Clinic Diet Phases

While there are two stages of the Mayo Clinic Diet, it's not a diet that has repeating cycles (such as six weeks on, one week off). There's just an introductory two-week stage dubbed "Lose it," followed by the second stage ("Live it"), which is ongoing.

The two-week "Lose it" stage dangles the promise of losing and keeping it off as much as 10 pounds. This can be accomplished by eliminating unhealthy habits such as watching TV while eating, consuming unhealthy snacks, eating too much meat, eating out quite often.

The Lose it! Phase

The "Lose It" phase lasts two weeks initially, but you can return to it anytime that you like. During this phase, you focus on 15 habits that Mayo Clinic researchers have identified as key to safe and healthy weight loss.

The goal is to add five healthy habits, break five unhealthy habits and adopt five bonus habits. Even though this phase is designed to jumpstart your weight loss, there's no calorie counting, and you can eat as many fruits and veggies as you want.

"The more habits you change, the more weight you will lose," says Dr Hensrud.

In fact, during the two-week "Lose It" period, you can safely drop between 6 and 10 pounds. "We believe the Lose It! phase is the healthiest way to quickly lose weight there is," the book asserts.

The healthy habits that you'll try to add are:

- Eating a healthy but moderately sized breakfast
- Eating vegetables and fruits
- Eating whole grains
- Eating healthy fats
- Exercising (including walking) for 30 minutes or more a day

Habits you'll try to ditch are:

- Eating added sugar
- Snacking on anything but fruits and veggies
- Eating a lot of meat or full-fat dairy
- Eating while watching TV
- Eating out, unless you can follow your eating plan's rules

Some of the bonus habits include: maintaining a diary of your foods, activity and goals, exercising more than an hour a day and eating minimally processed foods.

Live it! Phase

After the first two weeks, you transition to the "Live It" phase, focusing on lasting diet and lifestyle changes you can maintain in the long run. This phase, ideally, will last the rest of your life. From time to time, you can break some of the rules you followed in the "Lose It" phase, and you should still lose 1 to 2 pounds each week.

In the "Live It" phase, you estimate (without measuring) and count servings of food, rather than calories, which the program teaches you how to do. You try to eat a certain number of servings of certain types of food each day based on your personal program. You also exercise on a regular basis.

The Mayo Clinic Diet emphasizes making food choices to align with the Mayo Clinic healthy weight pyramid, with vegetables and fruit dominating the diet, followed by whole-grain carbohydrates, proteins and dairy, healthy fats and lastly sweets. For example, with a plan that allots 1,400 calories a day, you can eat four or more servings each of fruits and vegetables, five of carbs, four of dairy and/or protein and three of healthy fats. In addition to fruits and vegetables, some recommended foods are legumes, beans, whole-wheat flour and bran, nuts, salmon, tuna, avocados and olives.

"(The Mayo Clinic Diet) provides evidence-based advice," says Dr. Hensrud. He further claimed, "It's not effortless, but it's practical, realistic and enjoyable enough to be sustainable. It will not only help people manage their weight but improve their health in the process."

The Mayo Clinic Weight Pyramid For Weight Loss

The Mayo Clinic Healthy Weight Pyramid is divided into three sections that provide guidance on food and lifestyle choices. Fruits, vegetables, and physical activity make up the base of the pyramid, meaning these are the fundamentals of your diet and lifestyle.

Each layer upward gets smaller, representing less of what you're eating. Carbs comprise the next layer, followed by protein, fats, and finally, sweets.

While the pyramid defines carbs as breads and grains, note that certain starchy vegetables — like corn and potatoes — also count as carbs in this diet.

The diet encourages you to eat moderate portion sizes and teaches you how to plan your meals around its food pyramid, which has some resemblance to MyPlate guidelines — current nutrition guidelines, courtesy of the U.S.

Department of Agriculture (USDA) — which replaced the MyPyramid guide in 2011.

Both promote the intake of whole grains, a variety of vegetables, whole fruits, and low fat protein and dairy. They also encourage you to fill half your plate with fruits and veggies and limit your fat and sugar intake (1).

However, the Mayo Clinic Healthy Weight Pyramid also emphasizes exercise as an essential component of a healthier life — something MyPlate doesn't mention. In addition, since the Mayo Clinic Diet focuses on weight loss and maintenance, it recommends smaller portions than you may see in MyPlate and other food proportion tools.

What You Will Gain on The Mayo Clinic Diet

This diet is focused on promoting healthful foods like fruits and vegetables and whole grains, and it's also focused on helping you establish healthier habits.

The two-week "Lose It" phase may feel restrictive, but it can also jumpstart your weight loss. It's a short enough time to see some success and start making long-term lifestyle changes.

While the "Lose It" phase isn't sustainable long term, it can give people confidence. At first, when people start changing their habits, they are intimidated. Once they get into it and see they are losing weight, they become empowered. They're in it for the long haul.

So, if you want to push yourself for two weeks to see some progress, this diet might be a good choice for you. There's a good chance you'll lose weight because your eating habits have changed significantly, and that can be motivating to get you to the next phase, where you can figure out what works for you long-term.

This diet could be challenging if it's a complete overhaul of your eating habits or for people who don't want a low-calorie and low-fat approach. It's OK to feel like your health behavior is somewhat of a stretch. But it still has to feel like it can fit within your lifestyle.

And if the diet brings up any disordered eating habits, you might want to find a different approach.

PART II: The Mayo Clinic Diet

Much of the diet prioritizes restructuring how you eat rather than restricting entire food groups, so you won't have to say goodbye to all of your favorites just yet. During the "Live It!" phase, you'll need to eat certain amounts of servings in each food group to meet your calorie restrictions.

Dietary Recommendations on The Mayo Clinic Diet

- Vegetables: They're at the crux of this diet, and should be eaten whenever possible!

There are no rules on which kinds you may eat, or where they've come from, as long as they're largely unprocessed. You can eat anything from the fresh produce section or frozen varieties that may be easier on your budget.

- Fruits: Fresh is best, but you can also buy frozen and canned varieties as long as they're free of added sugar. The diet stipulates that you can have up to four ounces of pure fruit juice a day as well.

- Whole Grains: Again, unprocessed options are best here! Cereals, oatmeals, whole-grain bread, wheat pasta, and brown rice can all be part of your daily menu.

- Protein: It's not all about meat in the Mayo Clinic Diet when it comes to protein; you can also source beans and legumes and lean seafood, alongside eggs and tofu, too. Poultry and beef can also be enjoyed, especially if they're low-fat cuts or grinds.

- Fat-Free Dairy: Like yogurt, cheese, and low-fat or fat-free milk.

- Unsaturated Fats: Swap out other fatty items with things like heart-healthy olive oil, avocados, and plenty of nuts, among others.

Dietary Precautions on The Mayo Clinic Diet

Some diets can be difficult to stick to, causing people to lose motivation. Unlike many short-term options, the Mayo Clinic Diet aims to be a sustainable plan that you can follow for life. Rather than banning certain foods, it focuses on replacing unhealthy behaviors with ones that are more likely to support weight loss.

Foods you should limit or avoid on the Mayo Clinic Diet include:

- Fruits: fruits canned in syrup, more than 4 ounces (120 mL) a day of 100% fruit juice, and juice products that are not 100% fruit

- Vegetables: starchy vegetables, such as corn and potatoes — which count as carb choices

- Carbohydrates: white flour — such as in white breads and pastas — and refined sugars, such as table sugar

- Protein: meats high in saturated fats, such as ground beef and sausages

- Dairy: full fat milk, cheese, and yogurt

- Fats: saturated fats, such as those in egg yolks, butter, coconut oil, and red meats, as well as trans fats found in processed foods

- Sweets: more than 75 calories per day of candies, pastries, cookies, cake, or alcoholic beverages (during the first phase you should completely avoid this category)

PART III: THE MAYO CLINIC DIET RECIPES FOR EFFECTIVE WEIGHT LOSS

BREAKFAST RECIPES FOR WEIGHT LOSS

Panettone French toast

Ingredients

3 eggs

150ml whole milk

1 tsp mixed spice

2 tbsp double cream

3 tbsp brandy

40g unsalted butter

4 tbsp mixed dried fruit

4 slices panettone (around 320g), cut in half to make 8

60g crème fraîche, to serve

maple syrup, to serve (optional)

2 tsp icing sugar, to serve

Method

STEP 1

Tip the eggs, milk, mixed spice, double cream and 1 tbsp brandy into a jug and beat to combine, then pour the mixture into a large, shallow dish.

STEP 2

Pour the remaining brandy into a cold frying pan along with 15g butter and the mixed fruit. Warm over a low heat for 3-4 mins until the butter has melted and the liquid has thickened slightly. Pour the fruit mixture into a small heatproof bowl and set aside.

STEP 3

Lay the panettone slices in the egg mixture and flip over to soak. Do this quickly so it doesn't break apart. Set aside on a plate.

STEP 4

Melt the remaining butter over a medium-low heat in the frying pan you used earlier, and fry the panettone slices for 3-4 mins on each side until golden and cooked through. It's easier to do this over a lower heat so the outside doesn't burn before the centre cooks.

STEP 5

Divide the slices between four plates, then top with the crème fraîche, mixed fruit, a little maple syrup (if using) and a dusting of icing sugar.

Creamy mango & coconut smoothie

Ingredients

200ml (½ tall glass) coconut milk (we used Kara Dairy Free)

4 tbsp coconut milk yogurt (we used Coyo)

1 banana

1 tbsp ground flaxseed, sunflower and pumpkin seed (we used Linwoods)

120g (¼ bag) frozen mango chunks

1 passion fruit, to finish (optional)

Method

STEP 1

Measure all the **Ingredients** or use a tall glass for speed – they don't have to be exact. Put them into a blender and blitz until smooth. Pour into 1 tall glass (you'll have enough for a top up) or two short tumblers. Cut the passion fruit in half, if using, and scrape the seeds on top.

Spiced hot cross buns

Ingredients

For the dough

450g strong white flour, plus extra for dusting

2 x 7g sachets easy-blend yeast

50g caster sugar

150ml warm milk

1 egg, beaten

50g unsalted butter, melted, plus extra for greasing

oil, for greasing

The spices and dried fruit

1 tsp ground cinnamon

½ tsp mixed spice

¼ tsp grated nutmeg

100g currant

To decorate

4 tbsp plain flour

2 tbsp granulated sugar

Method

STEP 1

Put the flour, yeast, caster sugar and 1 tsp salt into a large mixing bowl with the spices and dried fruit and mix well. Make a well in the centre and pour in the warm milk, 50ml warm water, the beaten egg and the melted butter. Mix everything together to form a dough – start with a wooden spoon and finish with your hands. If the dough is too dry, add a little more warm water; if it's too wet, add more flour.

STEP 2

Knead in the bowl or on a floured surface until the dough becomes smooth and springy. Transfer to a clean, lightly greased bowl and cover loosely with a clean, damp tea towel. Leave in a warm place to rise until roughly doubled in size – this will take about 1 hr depending on how warm the room is.

STEP 3

Tip the risen dough onto a lightly floured surface. Knead for a few secs, then divide into 12 even portions – I roll my dough into a long sausage shape, then quarter and divide each quarter into 3 pieces. Shape each portion into a smooth round and place on a baking sheet greased with butter, leaving some room between each bun for it to rise.

STEP 4

Use a small, sharp knife to score a cross on the top of each bun, then cover with the damp tea towel again and leave in a warm place to prove for 20 mins until almost doubled in size again. Heat oven to 200C/180C fan/gas 6.

STEP 5

When the buns are ready to bake, mix the plain flour with just enough water to give you a thick paste. Spoon into a piping bag (or into a plastic food bag and snip the corner off) and pipe a white cross into the crosses you cut earlier. Bake for 12-15 mins until the buns are golden and sound hollow when tapped on the bottom. While still warm, melt the granulated sugar with 1 tbsp water in a small pan, then brush over the buns.

Tropical breakfast smoothie

Ingredients

3 passion fruits

1 banana, chopped

1small mango, peeled, stoned and chopped

300ml orange juice

ice cubes

Method

STEP 1

Scoop the pulp of the passion fruits into a blender and add the banana, mango and orange juice. Purée until smooth and drink immediately, topped with ice cubes.

Homemade muesli with oats, dates & berries

Ingredients

100g traditional oats

12 pecan nuts, broken into pieces

2 tbsp sunflower seeds

6 pitted medjool dates, snipped into pieces

25g high-fibre puffed wheat

4 x pots bio yogurt

300g mixed berries, such as raspberries, strawberries and blueberries

generous sprinkling of ground cinnamon (optional)

Method

STEP 1

Tip the oats into a frying pan and heat gently, stirring frequently until they are just starting to toast. Add the pecans and seeds to warm briefly, then tip into a large bowl and toss so they cool quickly.

STEP 2

Add the dates and puffed wheat, mix well until thoroughly combined, then serve topped with the yogurt and fruit, and a sprinkling of cinnamon, if you like.

Fluffy buckwheat pancakes

Ingredients

150g plain flour

150g buckwheat flour

2 tbsp caster sugar

1 tsp baking powder

1 tsp bicarbonate of soda

50g butter, melted

2 large eggs

400ml buttermilk

vegetable oil, for frying

To serve

blueberries

maple syrup

Method

STEP 1

Combine the plain flour, buckwheat flour, sugar, ½ tsp salt, baking powder and bicarbonate of soda in a large bowl. Combine the melted butter, eggs and buttermilk in a jug and whisk to combine. Stir the wet **Ingredients** slowly into the dry **Ingredients** until combined, to make a thick batter.

STEP 2

Heat a large non-stick pan or skillet over medium heat and brush with a light layer of vegetable oil. Add a few heaped tablespoons of the mixture into the pan and form into a circle. If your pan is large enough you can do 2-3 at a time, just don't overcrowd the pan too. Once the edges are set and bubbles appear on the surface (around 2-3 mins) flip and cook for a further 2 mins. The pancakes should be a deep golden brown on both sides.

Transfer to a warm oven on low and repeat the process until the batter is all used.

STEP 3

Serve stacked with fresh blueberries and maple syrup drizzled generously over the top.

Teacakes

Ingredients

100ml milk

30g butter

350g strong white bread flour

7g sachet fast action dried yeast

2 tbsp sugar

½ tsp mixed spice

75g mixed dried fruit (peel, sultanas, raisins and currants)

oil for greasing

1 egg, beaten

Method

STEP 1

Warm the milk with the butter in a pan until the butter has melted, then add 100ml water to cool the mixture to room temp. Tip the flour, yeast, sugar, spice and 1 tsp salt into a bowl, making sure the yeast is on the other side of the bowl to the salt. Make a well in the flour mixture and pour the milk and butter in, mixing until it forms big flakes, then bring together with your hands. Tip on a surface and knead until smooth (about 5 mins). Put the dough into a large, lightly oiled bowl, cover with a damp tea towel and leave until doubled in size, so about 1-1 ½ hours.

STEP 2

Line a tray with baking paper. Tip the mixed dried fruits into the dough and knead them in, trying to disperse them evenly throughout the dough. Cut your dough into 6 even-sized balls, take each ball and, using the cup of your hand, and pressing down a little with your palm, roll the ball in a circular motion on the surface to create tension across the top of the bun and a neat round shape. Place onto a tray about 5cm away from each other and press down with your palm to flatten the dough down a little, creating the teacake shape. Cover loosely with an oiled sheet of cling film, for a further 45 mins, or until they have doubled in size.

STEP 3

Meanwhile, heat the oven to 200C/180C fan/gas mark 6. Brush the top of each bun liberally with the egg wash, then bake for 20 mins on the top shelf of the oven, until the buns are golden and well risen. Allow to cool on a wire rack, then slice in half, toast and slather with butter if you like.

Shakshuka flatbread bake

Ingredients

For the shakshuka base

1 tbsp olive oil, for frying

1 small onion, finely chopped

2 garlic cloves, finely chopped

1 bay leaf

1 red chilli, finely chopped (deseeded if you don't like it very hot)

1 tsp cumin seeds

1 tsp smoked paprika

pinch cayenne pepper

1 red pepper, deseeded and sliced

400g can chopped tomatoes

200ml vegetable stock

small handful coriander, half finely chopped

For the flatbreads

2 flatbreads, roughly 20cm diameter (Turkish pide are good)

2 eggs

100g feta

Method

STEP 1

Heat the oil in a medium pan and fry the onions, garlic, bay leaf and chilli for 3 mins. Add the cumin, paprika and cayenne, season, then cook for a further 3 mins. Add the pepper and cook for 5 mins until it starts to soften.

STEP 2

Add the chopped tomatoes and stock, lower the heat and simmer for 20-25 mins until you have a thick ragu, then stir in the finely chopped coriander.

STEP 3

Heat oven to 180C/160C fan/gas 4. Lay each flatbread on a baking tray. Put half the vegetable mix in the centre of each and spread it out a bit, keeping at least an inch spare all the way around as a border. Make a small well in the centre and crack an egg on top of each flatbread. Crumble over the feta and put in the oven for 12-15 mins until the egg is set and the cheese melted slightly. Scatter over the remaining coriander and serve.

Baked oats

Ingredients

100g porridge oats

1 tsp baking powder

1 banana, peeled and chopped

1 tbsp maple syrup or honey

2 eggs

pinch of mixed spice or ground cinnamon

100g chocolate chips, blueberries or raspberries, plus extra to serve flavourless oil, for the ramekins

Method

STEP 1

Heat the oven to 180C/160C fan/gas 4. Put the oats in a blender and pulse a few times until they start to resemble flour. Add the baking powder, chopped banana, maple syrup or honey, eggs and mixed spice or cinnamon, and whizz until smooth. Stir in the chocolate chips or berries.

STEP 2

Lightly oil four heatproof ramekins, then divide the batter between them. Bake for 20-25 mins, or until well-risen and the baked oats spring back when lightly pressed. Scatter with more chocolate chips or berries before serving, if you like.

Vegan baked oats

Ingredients

150g porridge oats

2 tsp vanilla extract

225ml unsweetened almond milk, plus extra to serve (optional)

1 large, very ripe banana, peeled

185g frozen mixed berries (ours had a combination of strawberries, blackberries and currants)

1 tsp maple syrup (optional)

1-2 tbsp toasted flaked almonds

Method

STEP 1

Heat the oven to 190C/170C fan/ gas 5. Tip the oats into a heatproof bowl, then pour over 450ml boiling water from the kettle. Stir well, then stir in the vanilla and almond milk.

STEP 2

Mash the banana, then spread over the base of a medium baking dish (ours was a 20 x 28cm oval) and stir in the frozen fruit to fully combine. You want the banana to sweeten the berries, but you can add 1 tsp maple syrup, if you like. Pour over the oat mixture and scatter with the almonds. Bake for

30-40 mins until set and the fruit juices are bubbling at the edges of the dish. Scoop into bowls and serve with a little extra milk, if you like.

Date & buckwheat granola with pecans & seeds

Ingredients

For the granola

85g buckwheat

4 medjool dates, stoned

1 tsp ground cinnamon

100g traditional oats

2 tsp rapeseed oil

25g sunflower seeds

25g pumpkin seeds

25g flaked almonds

50g pecan nuts, roughly broken into halves

50g sultanas (without added oil)

For the yogurt & fruit (to serve 2)

2 x 150ml pots low-fat bio natural yogurt

2 ripe nectarines or peaches, stoned and sliced

Method

STEP 1

Soak the buckwheat overnight in cold water. The next day, drain and rinse the buckwheat. Put the dates in a pan with 300ml water and the cinnamon, and blitz with a stick blender until completely smooth. Add the buckwheat, bring to the boil and cook, uncovered, for 5 mins until pulpy. Meanwhile, heat oven to 150C/130C fan/gas 2 and line two large baking trays with baking parchment.

STEP 2

Stir the oats and oil into the date and buckwheat mixture, then spoon small clusters of the mixture onto the baking trays. Bake for 15 mins, then carefully scrape the clusters from the parchment if they have stuck and turn before spreading out again. Return to the oven for another 15 mins, turning frequently, until firm and golden.

STEP 3

When the mix is dry enough, tip into a bowl, mix in the seeds and nuts with the sultanas and toss well. When cool, serve each person a generous handful with yogurt and fruit, and pack the excess into an airtight container. Will keep for a week. On other days you can vary the fruit or serve with milk or a dairy-free alternative instead of the yogurt.

Leftover porridge pancakes

Ingredients

150g cold leftover porridge

150g self-raising flour

2 tsp baking powder

1 ripe banana, mashed

2 large eggs

100ml milk

2 tsp vegetable or sunflower oil

fruit, yogurt and maple syrup or honey, to serve

Method

STEP 1

Mix the porridge, flour, baking powder, banana, eggs and milk in a bowl. Heat the oil in a frying pan. Drop 2-3 tbsp of the porridge mixture into the pan and cook over a medium heat until the underside is golden and bubbles are popping on the surface.

STEP 2

Flip over and cook for another few mins until cooked through, then keep warm in a low oven and repeat until you've used up all the batter. Serve with the fruit and yogurt and top with a drizzle of the syrup or honey.

Cinnamon crêpes with nut butter, sliced banana & raspberries

Ingredients

75g gluten-free brown bread flour

1 tsp ground cinnamon

1 medium egg

225ml semi-skimmed milk

1 tsp rapeseed oil, for frying

2 tbsp almond nut butter (make your own with recipe in 'goes well with', right)

1 banana, sliced

140g raspberries

lemon wedges

Method

STEP 1

Tip the flour into a large mixing bowl with the cinnamon. Add the egg and milk, and whisk vigorously until you have a smooth pouring consistency.

STEP 2

Place a non-stick frying pan over a medium heat and add a little of the oil. When the oil starts to heat, wipe most of it away with kitchen paper. Once the pan is hot, pour a small amount of the batter into the centre of the pan and swirl it to the sides of the pan in a thin layer. Leave to cook, untouched, for about 2 mins. When it is brown underneath, turn over and cook for 1 min more.

STEP 3

Transfer to a warm plate and cover with foil to keep warm. Repeat with the remaining batter. Divide the warm pancakes between 2 plates and serve with the nut butter, banana, raspberries and lemon to assemble at the table.

Raspberry and apple smoothie

Ingredients

2 apples, cored (we used Granny Smith)

150g frozen raspberries

150ml natural yogurt

2 tbsp porridge oats

½ lemon, juiced

100ml milk

Method

STEP 1

Tip all **Ingredients** into a blender or smoothie maker and blitz until smooth, adding 50ml water or milk if it's too thick.

Creamy mushrooms on toast

Ingredients

1 slice wholemeal bread

1 ½ tbsp light cream cheese

1 tsp rapeseed oil

3handfuls sliced, small flat mushrooms

2 tbsp skimmed milk

¼ tsp wholegrain mustard

1 tbsp snipped chives

Method

STEP 1

Toast the bread, then spread with a little of the cream cheese.

STEP 2

Meanwhile, heat the oil in a non-stick pan and cook the mushrooms, stirring frequently, until softened. Spoon in the milk, remaining cheese and the mustard. Stir well until coated. Tip onto the toast and top with chives.

Stollen muffins

Ingredients

200g plain flour

50g ground almonds

1 tsp baking powder

1 tsp bicarbonate of soda

½ tsp ground cinnamon

100g golden caster sugar

100g marzipan, diced

25g pistachios, roughly chopped

50g toasted flaked almonds

25g sultanas or raisins

50g dried cherries or cranberries

50g dried apricots, diced

2 large eggs

100g unsalted butter, melted and cooled

125ml full-fat natural yogurt

1 tsp almond extract

2 tbsp icing sugar

You will need

12 paper muffin cases (we used tulip cases)

Method

STEP 1

Heat oven to 220C/200C fan/gas 7 and put the muffin cases in a 12-hole muffin tin. Mix the flour, ground almonds, baking powder, bicarb, 1/4 tsp cinnamon, the sugar, marzipan, nuts and dried fruit in a mixing bowl. Whisk together the eggs, melted butter, yogurt and almond extract, then pour over the dry **Ingredients** and very quickly mix with a wooden spoon until the mixture has just come together – the most important thing is to not overmix – don't worry if there are still a few floury bits.

STEP 2

Quickly divide the mix between the cases and put in the oven on the top shelf. Bake for 5 mins, then lower the heat to 180C/160C fan/gas 4 and bake for 15 mins more until they are risen, golden, and a skewer inserted into the middle of them comes out clean.

STEP 3

Once they have cooled a little and are firm enough to handle, lift out of the tin onto wire racks and cool for 5 mins. Mix the icing sugar with the remaining 1/4 tsp cinnamon and sieve over the muffins. Serve warm. Will keep for 3 days in an airtight container.

Amaranth porridge with green tea & ginger compote

Ingredients

For the compote

8 ready-to-eat dried apricots, about 50g/2oz

25g dried cherries

2 tsp shredded fresh ginger

2 green tea teabags

1 red skinned apple

4 tbsp fresh pomegranate seeds

For the porridge

85g amaranth

2 tbsp chia seeds

2 x 150g pots bio plain yogurt, or dairy-free alternative

Method

STEP 1

The night before having this for breakfast, put the dried apricots and cherries in a pan with the ginger shreds, pour in 350ml water then cover the pan and bring to the boil. Simmer for 10 mins then turn off the heat, add the tea bags and allow to infuse for 2 mins. Remove the bags and squeeze the excess liquid from them back into the pan. Rinse the amaranth in a sieve under a cold running tap to remove the saponins (natural compounds that leave a slightly bitter taste). Tip the amaranth into a small pan, pour in 325ml water, cover and set aside.

STEP 2

The next morning, bring the pan with the amaranth to the boil, turn down the heat then cover the pan and cook for 10-15 mins until the grains are tender and the liquid has been absorbed. Stir in the chia seeds.

STEP 3

Stir half the yogurt into the mix to make a porridge consistency and spoon into shallow bowls. Top with the remaining yogurt. Core and slice the apple into the compote and spoon on to the porridge and scatter with the pomegranate seeds.

Slow cooker rice pudding

Ingredients

1 tsp butter

1l semi-skimmed milk

200g wholegrain rice

nutmeg or cinnamon

1 tbsp honey, a handful toasted, flaked almonds and fruit, to serve

Method

STEP 1

Butter the slow cooker all over the base and half way up the sides. Heat the milk to simmering point. Mix the pudding rice with the milk and pour it into the slow cooker. Add a grating of nutmeg or cinnamon. Cook for 2½ hours on High and stir once or twice if you can.

STEP 2

Serve with honey, or flaked almonds and fruit if you like.

Black bean & barley cakes with poached eggs

Ingredients

2 x 400g cans black beans, drained well

15g porridge oats

2 tsp ground coriander

1 tsp cumin seeds

2 tsp thyme leaves

1 tsp vegetable bouillon powder

5 large eggs

2 spring onions, the white part finely chopped, the green thinly sliced

400g can barley, drained

2-3 tsp rapeseed oil

200g pack cherry tomatoes on the vine

4 tbsp sunflower seeds

Method

STEP 1

Tip the beans, oats, ground coriander, cumin seeds, thyme and vegetable bouillon powder into a bowl and blitz together with a hand blender to make a rough paste. Stir in 1 egg with the whites of the spring onion and barley. If you're following our Healthy Diet Plan, separate half the mix for another morning and chill.

STEP 2

Heat half the oil in your largest frying pan and fry the other half of the mixture in two big spoonfuls, gently pressed to make flat cakes. After 7 mins, carefully turn over to cook the other side for 4-5 mins.

STEP 3

Meanwhile, poach two eggs in a pan of boiling water for 3-4 mins, and gently fry half of the tomatoes on the vine in a little oil for a few mins to brown slightly. Slide the cakes onto plates and top with the tomatoes, eggs, a scattering of the spring onion greens and half the sun ower seeds. On another morning, repeat steps 2 and 3 with the remaining ingredients.

STEP 4

If you're not following the Healthy Diet Plan and you're serving four, follow steps 2 and 3 with all the **Ingredients** instead of only half.

LUNCH RECIPES FOR WEIGHT LOSS

Vegan burritos

Ingredients

4 large or 8 small tortilla wraps

2 large handfuls spinach leaves, shredded

1 avocado, thinly sliced (optional)

hot sauce, to serve

For the chipotle black beans

1 tbsp oil

1 garlic clove, crushed

1 tbsp chipotle paste

400g can chopped tomatoes

400g black beans, drained

1 bunch coriander, chopped

For the lime and red onion rice

250g wholegrain rice, cooked and drained

1 lime, juiced

½ red onion, very finely chopped

50g hazelnuts, roughly chopped

Method

STEP 1

To make the beans, heat the oil in a pan and fry the garlic for a minute, then stir in the chipotle paste. Tip in the tomatoes, stir and bring to a simmer. Season with salt. Simmer until thick, add the beans and cook briefly (make sure any water gets cooked off), then stir in the coriander.

STEP 2

If you are using cold cooked rice, then warm it through, stir in the lime juice, red onion and nuts and season well.

STEP 3

Lay out the tortillas and sprinkle over some spinach, add some avocado slices and some rice, then top with the bean mix. Add a shake of hot sauce, if you like. Roll the bottom up, then fold the sides in to stop the filling falling out as you roll. Wrap tightly in foil, if you like, and cut in half.

Beef stew & dumplings

Ingredients

For the stew

1 tbsp rapeseed oil

2 medium onions, chopped

2 bay leaves

4 thyme sprigs, plus extra leaves to serve

550g chunks of lean braising steak

100ml red wine

1 ½ tbsp plain flour

1 tsp English mustard powder

230g can plum tomatoes

500ml vegetable bouillon

280g carrots, halved lengthways and sliced

400g piece butternut squash, deseeded, peeled and cut into 3-4cm/11/4-11/2in chunks

140g chestnut mushrooms, quartered or halved if large

For the dumplings

140g self-raising flour

½ tsp English mustard powder

2 spring onions, ends trimmed, finely chopped

3 tbsp chopped parsley

2 tbsp rapeseed oil

100ml buttermilk

Method

STEP 1

Heat the oil in a large saucepan or deep sauté pan. Tip in the onions, bay leaves and thyme sprigs, and fry over a medium heat for about 8 mins, stirring often, until the onions are turning golden. Raise the heat, add the steak and stir-fry briefly until it starts to lose its raw, red colour. Pour in the wine, stir to deglaze the brown sticky bits from the bottom of the pan, and let it bubble briefly. Lower the heat, sprinkle in the flour and mustard powder, and stir for 1 min. The meat should now be coated in a thick, rich sauce.

STEP 2

Mix in the tomatoes, stirring to break them down. Stir in the stock and bring to the boil. Tip in the carrots, squash and mushrooms, lower the heat, cover with a lid and leave to simmer gently for 1 hr 40 mins, stirring occasionally. Uncover and cook for a further 20 mins, still on a gentle simmer, until the meat is very tender. Season with pepper.

STEP 3

When the stew is nearly cooked, heat oven to 190C/170C fan/gas 5. Put a 2.25-litre casserole dish in to heat it up. Meanwhile, make the dumplings. Put the flour, mustard powder, some pepper and a pinch of salt in a bowl, then stir in the spring onions and parsley. Mix the oil and buttermilk together and gently stir into the flour. Add a drop or two of cold water, if needed, to pick up any dry bits on the bottom of the bowl, and stir to make a soft and slightly sticky dough. Be as light-handed as you can, as overmixing or overhandling will toughen the dumplings. Cut the dough into 8 pieces and very lightly shape each into a small, rough ball.

STEP 4

Carefully transfer the stew to the hot casserole dish and remove the bay leaves and thyme sprigs. Sit the dumplings on top and press them down into the gravy to very slightly submerge. Put the dish on a baking sheet and cook for about 20 mins until the dumplings have risen and are golden on top. Serve with a light scattering of thyme leaves.

Vegan chickpea curry jacket potatoes

Ingredients

4 sweet potatoes

1 tbsp coconut oil

1 ½ tsp cumin seeds

1 large onion, diced

2 garlic cloves, crushed

thumb-sized piece ginger, finely grated

1 green chilli, finely chopped

1 tsp garam masala

1 tsp ground coriander

½ tsp turmeric

2 tbsp tikka masala paste

2 x 400g can chopped tomatoes

2 x 400g can chickpeas, drained

lemon wedges and coriander leaves, to serve

Method

STEP 1

Heat oven to 200C/180C fan/gas 6. Prick the sweet
potatoes all over with a fork, then put on a baking

tray and roast in the oven for 45 mins or until tender when pierced with a knife.

STEP 2

Meanwhile, melt the coconut oil in a large saucepan over medium heat. Add the cumin seeds and fry for 1 min until fragrant, then add the onion and fry for 7-10 mins until softened.

STEP 3

Put the garlic, ginger and green chilli into the pan, and cook for 2-3 mins. Add the spices and tikka masala paste and cook for a further 2 mins until fragrant, then tip in the tomatoes. Bring to a simmer, then tip in the chickpeas and cook for a further 20 mins until thickened. Season.

STEP 4

Put the roasted sweet potatoes on four plates and cut open lengthways. Spoon over the chickpea curry and squeeze over the lemon wedges. Season, then scatter with coriander before serving.

Spring tabbouleh

Ingredients

6 tbsp olive oil

1 tbsp garam masala

2 x 400g cans chickpeas, drained and rinsed

250g ready-to-eat mixed grain pouch

250g frozen peas

2 lemons, zested and juiced

large pack parsley, leaves roughly chopped

large pack mint, leaves roughly chopped

250g radishes, roughly chopped

1 cucumber, chopped

pomegranate seeds, to serve

Method

STEP 1

Heat oven to 200C/180C fan/ gas 6. Mix 4 tbsp oil with the garam masala and some seasoning. Toss with the chickpeas in a large roasting tin, then cook for 15 mins until starting to crisp. Tip in the mixed grains, peas and lemon zest. Mix well, then return to the oven for about 10 mins until warmed through.

STEP 2

Transfer to a large bowl or platter, then toss through the herbs, radishes, cucumber, remaining oil and lemon juice. Season to taste and scatter over the pomegranate seeds. Any leftovers will be good for lunch the next day.

Peanut hummus with fruit & veg sticks

Ingredients

380g carton chickpeas

zest and juice 0.5 lemon (use the other 1/2 to squeeze over the apple to stop it browning, if you like)

1 tbsp tahini

0.5-1 tsp smoked paprika

2 tbsp roasted unsalted peanuts

1 tsp rapeseed oil

2 crisp red apples, cored and cut into slices

2 carrots, cut into sticks

4 celery sticks, cut into batons lengthways

Method

STEP 1

Drain the chickpeas, reserving the liquid. Tip three-quarters of the chickpeas into a food processor and add the lemon zest and juice, tahini, paprika, peanuts and oil with 3 tbsp chickpea liquid. Blitz in a food processor until smooth, then stir in the reserved chickpeas. Serve with the fruit and veg sticks.

Halloumi, carrot & orange salad

Ingredients

2 large oranges

1½ tbsp wholegrain mustard

1½ tsp honey

1 tbsp white wine vinegar

3 tbsp rapeseed or olive oil, plus extra for frying

2 large carrots, peeled

225g block halloumi, sliced

100g bag watercress or baby spinach

Method

STEP 1

Cut the peel and pith away from the oranges. Use a small serrated knife to segment the orange, catching any juices in a bowl, then squeeze any excess juice from the off-cut pith into the bowl as well. Add the mustard, honey, vinegar, oil and some seasoning to the bowl and mix well.

STEP 2

Using a vegetable peeler, peel carrot ribbons into the dressing bowl and toss gently. Heat a drizzle of oil in a frying pan and cook the halloumi for a few mins until golden on both sides. Toss the watercress through the dressed carrots. Arrange the watercress mixture on plates and top with the halloumi and oranges.

Carrot & parsnip soup

Ingredients

½ tbsp olive oil

2 onions, finely chopped

2 celery sticks, finely chopped

2 garlic cloves, crushed

½ small bunch thyme, leaves picked

3 large carrots, peeled and roughly chopped

2 large parsnips, peeled and roughly chopped

1 litre vegetable stock

100ml double cream

¼ bunch parsley, finely chopped (optional)

Method

STEP 1

Heat the oil in a large saucepan and fry the onion and celery for 10 mins, stirring occasionally until softened. If they start to catch, add a small splash of water. Add the garlic, thyme and ½ tsp black pepper and cook for 2 mins. Add the carrots, parsnips and stock and bring to the boil. Reduce to a simmer and cook for 20 mins until the vegetables are soft, stirring occasionally.

STEP 2

Blend using a stick blender until smooth. Add the cream and blitz again until combined, then taste for seasoning. To serve, ladle into bowls and scatter over a little chopped parsley, if you like.

Seared red mullet with à la Grecque vegetables & basmati pilaf

Ingredients

4 red mullet about 300g each, ungutted, scaled (see step by step)

2large banana shallots or 4 smaller ones

2 fat garlic cloves

2 carrots

1 fennel bulb

about olive oil

good pinch saffron strands

3 cardamom pods

1 bay leaf

250g cherry tomato, halved

100ml balsamic vinegar

large handful fresh coriander, roughly chopped

For the pilaf

250g basmati rice

1 orange, grated zest

1 lemon, grated zest

1 lime, grated zest

1 tsp fenugreek seed, crushed

½ tsp coriander seeds, crushed

½ tsp fennel seeds, crushed

2 cardamom pods, crushed

1 cinnamon stick

4 star anise

2 tbsp olive oil

1 onion, sliced

150ml dry white wine

450ml fish stock (made with the bones or use a good-quality ready made stock)

Method

STEP 1

Using a very sharp filleting knife, make a cut at the head on a slant, then turn the fish and cut under the dorsal (top) fin.

STEP 2

Press the fish down firmly with one hand, bending it slightly along the back so that the flesh is taut. Then slide the knife in at the top of the backbone.

STEP 3

Cut down against the rib cage at a downward slant. Letting the knife do the work, push the tip against the centre of the bone, working your way down to the tail. Turn the fish over and repeat on the other side.

STEP 4

Trim the fillets neatly. Remove the pin bones using your fingernails or tweezers. In the restaurant kitchen, we use a straight-sided potato peeler, hooking the bone head and twisting it out. After filleting and pin-boning, pat dry (do not rinse or you'll lose flavour).

STEP 5

Thinly slice the shallots, garlic and carrots. Quarter and core the fennel then slice the fennel quarters as thinly as you can – use a mandolin, if possible.

STEP 6

Heat 3 tbsp oil in a sauté frying pan and fry the vegetables together for 5 mins with the saffron, cardamom and bay leaf.

STEP 7

Add 2 tbsp oil and continue cooking for 5 mins. Season well, remove from the heat and stir in the tomatoes, vinegar, 3 tbsp oil, and coriander.

STEP 8

Heat 2 tbsp oil in a non-stick frying pan and, when hot, lay in the fillets, skin-side down. Season and cook for 2 mins, then carefully turn and cook for 1-

2 mins – but no more, the flesh should be slightly undercooked. Remove from the heat.

STEP 9

Tip half the vegetables into a shallow dish, lay the fillets on top, then cover with the remaining vegetables.

STEP 10

Leave to marinate for 10 mins before serving warm. Prepare up to this point up to 1 day ahead and keep in the fridge. Bring to room temperature before serving.

STEP 11

Soak the rice in cold water for 5 mins, then drain well and tip into a bowl. Mix in the grated zests. Add all the spices. Heat oven to 200C/fan 180C/gas 6. Make a cartouche (see tip below).

STEP 12

Heat oil in an ovenproof casserole, then sauté onion for 5 mins. Add rice and wine, boil until evaporated, then add the stock. Bring to the boil.

STEP 13

Top with the cartouche and a well-fitting lid. Bake for 20 mins, then take out of the oven, uncover, fork the grains, re-cover. Leave to stand for 5 mins, then serve.

Thai green chicken curry

Ingredients

225g new potatoes, cut into chunks

100g green beans, trimmed and halved

1 tbsp vegetable or sunflower oil

1 garlic clove, chopped

1 rounded tbsp or 4 tsp Thai green curry paste (you can't fit the tablespoon into some of the jars)

400ml can coconut milk

2 tsp Thai fish sauce

1 tsp caster sugar

450g boneless skinless chicken (breasts or thighs), cut into bite-size pieces

2 lime leaves finely shredded, or 3 wide strips lime zest, plus extra to garnish

good handful of basil leaves

boiled rice, to serve

Method

STEP 1

Put 225g new potatoes, cut into chunks, in a pan of boiling water and cook for 5 minutes.

STEP 2

Add 100g trimmed and halved green beans and cook for a further 3 minutes, by which time both should be just tender but not too soft. Drain and put to one side.

STEP 3

In a wok or large frying pan, heat 1 tbsp vegetable or sunflower oil until very hot, then drop in 1 chopped garlic clove and cook until golden, this should take only a few seconds. Don't let it go very dark or it will spoil the taste.

STEP 4

Spoon in 1 rounded tbsp Thai green curry paste and stir it around for a few seconds to begin to cook the spices and release all the flavours.

STEP 5

Next, pour in a 400ml can of coconut milk and let it come to a bubble.

STEP 6

Stir in 2 tsp Thai fish sauce and 1 tsp caster sugar, then 450g bite-size chicken pieces. Turn the heat down to a simmer and cook, covered, for about 8 minutes until the chicken is cooked.

STEP 7

Tip in the potatoes and beans and let them warm through in the hot coconut milk, then add 2 finely shredded lime leaves (or 3 wide strips lime zest).

STEP 8

Add a good handful basil leaves, but only leave them briefly on the heat or they will quickly lose their brightness.

STEP 9

Scatter with lime to garnish and serve immediately with boiled rice.

Chicken enchiladas

Ingredients

3 tbsp olive oil

2 red onions, sliced

2 red peppers, sliced

3 red chillies, 2 deseeded and chopped, 1 sliced

small bunch coriander, stalks finely chopped, leaves roughly chopped - plus extra to serve (optional)

2 garlic cloves, crushed

1 tbsp ground coriander

1 tbsp cumin seeds

6 skinless chicken breasts, cut into small chunks

415g can refried beans (we used Discovery)

198g can sweetcorn, drained

700ml bottle passata

1 tsp golden caster sugar

10 tortillas

2 x 142ml pots soured cream

200g cheddar, grated

Method

STEP 1

Heat 2 tbsp of the oil in your largest pan, then fry the onions, peppers, chopped chilli and coriander stalks with half the garlic for 10 mins until soft. Stir in 2 tsp ground coriander and 2 tsp cumin seeds, then fry for 1 min more. Meanwhile, in another frying pan, fry the chicken in the remaining oil, in batches, until browned – add it to the pan of veg as it is done.

STEP 2

Stir the beans, sweetcorn, coriander leaves and 150ml of the passata into the veg and chicken. In a bowl, mix the rest of the passata with the other crushed garlic clove, the remaining spices and the sugar, then set aside.

STEP 3

To assemble, lay the tortillas onto a board and divide the chicken mixture between them, folding over the ends and rolling up to seal. Divide the passata sauce into the dishes you are using, then top with the enchiladas. Dot over the soured cream, sprinkle with grated cheese and scatter with the sliced chilli.

STEP 4

Cool and freeze (see freezing tips, below) or, if eating straight away, heat oven to 200C/180C fan/gas 6, then bake for 30 mins, scattering with more coriander leaves to serve, if you like.

Vegetable phat Thai

Ingredients

200g pack thick rice noodles (see KNOW-HOW)

bunch coriander

2 garlic cloves

3cm piece fresh root ginger, peeled

1 tbsp vegetable oil

1 yellow pepper, thinly sliced

140g sugar snap peas

1 egg, beaten

1 red chilli, deseeded and finey chopped

1 tbsp caster sugar

3 tbsp fish sauce

2 tbsp oyster sauce

100g beansprouts

juice 1 lime

50g roasted peanuts, roughly chopped

bunch spring onions, thinly sliced

Method

STEP 1

If using dried noodles, soak according to pack instructions. Cut the stalks off the coriander and finely chop them (set the leaves aside for later). Tip the chopped stalks into a mortar along with the garlic and ginger, then pound to form an aromatic paste.

STEP 2

Heat a wok and, when smoking, tip in the oil, then the paste. Cook for a few secs, then stir in the pepper and peas. Cook a few mins more until softened, then pour in the egg and chilli. Stir around the pan until cooked, then add the sugar, fish and oyster sauces. Drain the noodles, then add to the pan. Toss everything together, adding a little water if the noodles seem a bit dry. Just before serving, stir in the beansprouts and lime juice, then place on a serving plate and scatter over the roasted peanuts, spring onions and coriander leaves.

Teriyaki steak with pak choi & noodles

Ingredients

½ tsp Chinese five-spice powder

2 lean beef steak, 175g each

1 tbsp sunflower oil

2 pak choi, trimmed and quartered

1 medium carrot, thinly sliced

1 red pepper, deseeded and thinly sliced

150g pack straight-to-wok egg noodles

3 tbsp teriyaki sauce

Method

STEP 1

Mix the five-spice with 1/2 tsp flaky sea salt and 1/2 tsp black pepper, and rub into the steaks. Heat 1 tsp of the oil in a large, non-stick frying pan over a medium-high heat. Fry the steak for 4-5 mins each side or until done to your liking. Transfer to a warmed plate, cover loosely with foil and leave to rest.

STEP 2

Pour the remaining oil into the pan, add the pak choi, the carrot and pepper. Stir-fry for 3 mins, then add the noodles and stir-fry for 2 mins more.

STEP 3

Pour in the teriyaki sauce and simmer for a few secs, then divide the vegetable noodles between 2 warmed plates or shallow bowls. Slice the steak thickly and place on top.

Fruity tabbouleh with feta

Ingredients

100g bulgur wheat

6 tbsp olive oil

100g couscous

200g mixed shelled nut, roughly chopped (any mixture of almonds, hazelnuts, walnuts, pecans and pistachios)

200g mixed dried fruit, large fruit chopped (any mixture of raisins, sultanas, apricots, dates and cranberries)

zest and juice 2 lemons

small pack mint, leaves roughly chopped

small pack flat-leaf parsley, leaves roughly chopped

2 garlic cloves, crushed

100g feta cheese, crumbled

grilled lamb or pork chops, to serve (optional)

Method

STEP 1

Boil the kettle. Put the bulgur wheat in a sieve and rinse with cold water until the water runs clear. Drain well and transfer to a mixing bowl. Pour over 200ml boiling water and 1 tbsp olive oil, cover with a plate and leave to soak for 30 mins. Meanwhile, put the couscous into a second mixing bowl with 1 tbsp olive oil, just cover with boiling water, then cover with a plate and leave to stand for 5-10 mins.

STEP 2

Once the bulgur wheat and couscous are ready, put them in a mixing bowl and fluff up the grains with a fork. Stir through the nuts and dried fruit, too.

STEP 3

Whisk together the lemon zest and juice, herbs, remaining olive oil and the garlic. Pour over the grains, nuts and fruit, and stir everything together well with some seasoning. Transfer to a serving plate, scatter with the crumbled feta, and serve with grilled lamb or pork chops, if you like.

Lemon roast poussin with spring vegetables

Ingredients

2 oven-ready poussin

2 garlic cloves, smashed but left whole

small bunch thyme

1 lemon, halved (use the zest for the vegetables)

25g butter, softened

For the braised peas & lettuce

1 tbsp olive oil

150g smoked streaky bacon, preferably in one piece, cut into small chunks

150g pearl onions, halved

150ml fresh chicken stock

200g frozen petits pois

1 Baby Gem lettuce, shredded

For the spring vegetables

8 baby courgettes, sliced in half lengthways

200g baby carrot, trimmed, halved on the diagonal if large

10 baby leeks, trimmed

1 tbsp olive oil

1 tsp balsamic vinegar

zest 1 lemon

8 radishes, halved or quartered if large

Method

STEP 1

Heat oven to 220C/fan 200C/ gas 7. Season the inside of the poussins generously with salt and pepper, then stuff each with a garlic clove, half a bunch of thyme and a lemon half.

STEP 2

Sit the birds in a shallow roasting dish. Smother generously with butter, then season the skin with sea salt and black pepper. Roast in the oven for about 40 mins.

STEP 3

While the birds are roasting, prepare the accompaniments. For the braised peas and lettuce, heat a frying pan and add a drizzle of oil. Sizzle the bacon for 2 mins until starting to crisp. Turn down the heat a little, toss in the onions, then continue to cook for 6-7 mins until they are golden.

STEP 4

Pour the chicken stock into the pan, simmer for 2 mins, then scatter in the peas and cook for 2 mins more. Lastly, stir in the lettuce and cook for 1 min until just wilted, then set aside.

STEP 5

For the spring vegetables, bring a large pan of salted water to the boil and have a bowl of iced water at the ready. In batches, boil all the veg (except the radishes), then transfer to the iced water. The courgettes will take 3 mins, the carrots and leeks 2 mins. Drain the vegetables, then lay them on kitchen paper to dry.

STEP 6

Heat a drizzle of olive oil in another frying pan, then stir-fry the vegetables until just starting to colour. Add the vinegar, lemon zest and a little seasoning. Turn off the heat, toss through the radishes, then drizzle with a little more oil.

STEP 7

Check if the poussins are cooked by inserting a skewer or small knife between the leg and the breast; if the juices are pink, give the bird an extra 5-10 minutes in the oven. Once ready, remove the poussins from the dish and leave to rest, upside down, for 10 mins (this keeps the breasts from drying out). To make a simple gravy, remove the lemon halves from the poussins, squeeze into the juices in the roasting dish, then whisk together.

STEP 8

Strain the lemony juices into a jug. You are now ready to carve the birds and plate up.

STEP 9

Using a sharp knife, cut through the thigh joint and remove the leg. Cut each leg through the joint to separate the drumstick from the thigh. Carefully carve the breasts away from the bone, cutting through the joint to leave the wing attached. Carve each breast into 2 pieces so each portion has 2 pieces of leg and 2 pieces of breast.

STEP 10

Spoon a mound of the braised peas and lettuce into the centre of 4 large, shallow, bowls. Neatly assemble a 'nest' of vegetables around the lettuce. Pile the carved poussin on top of the lettuce, giving each serving the same amount of meat. Pour over the lemony sauce and serve straight away.

Tomato & courgette risotto

Ingredients

2 tbsp olive oil

1 small onion, diced

2 garlic cloves, crushed

½ tsp coriander seeds, crushed

200g risotto rice

500ml vegetable stock

200g carton passata

12 cherry tomatoes, halved

2 courgettes, halved and sliced

2 tbsp mascarpone

parmesan (or vegetarian alternative), grated, to serve

Method

STEP 1

Put1 tbsp of oil in a large pan over a medium heat. Add the onion and cook for 5-7 mins until softened. Add the garlic and coriander seeds and cook, stirring, for another 1 min. Stir in the risotto rice, coating it in the onion mixture. Gradually add 300ml of the vegetable stock, stirring until fully absorbed by the rice between each addition. Pour the passata into the risotto, cover and simmer for 10-15 mins. Stir occasionally and add more stock as needed.

STEP 2

Meanwhile, heat oven to 200C/180C fan/gas 6. Put the cherry tomatoes and courgettes in a roasting tin, keeping them separate, drizzle with 1 tbsp olive oil, season and roast for 10-12 mins until just tender.

STEP 3

Add the mascarpone and plenty of seasoning to the risotto. Stir until the rice is completely cooked and the risotto is creamy, about 5 mins more. Add the courgettes and stir to combine. Serve the risotto in bowls topped with the roasted tomatoes and some grated Parmesan.

Minty griddled chicken & peach salad

Ingredients

1 lime, zested and juiced

1 tbsp rapeseed oil

2 tbsp mint, finely chopped, plus a few leaves to serve

1 garlic clove, finely grated

2 skinless chicken breast fillets (300g)

160g fine beans, trimmed and halved

2 peaches (200g), each cut into 8 thick wedges

1 red onion, cut into wedges

1 large Little Gem lettuce (165g), roughly shredded

½ x 60g pack rocket

1 small avocado, stoned and sliced

240g cooked new potatoes

Method

STEP 1

Mix the lime zest and juice, oil and mint, then put half in a bowl with the garlic. Thickly slice the chicken at a slight angle, add to the garlic mixture and toss together with plenty of black pepper.

STEP 2

Cook the beans in a pan of water for 3-4 mins until just tender. Meanwhile, griddle the chicken and onion for a few mins each side until cooked and tender. Transfer to a plate, then quickly griddle the peaches. If you don't have a griddle pan, use a non-stick frying pan with a drop of oil.

STEP 3

Toss the warm beans and onion in the remaining mint mixture, and pile onto a platter or into individual shallow bowls with the lettuce and rocket. Top with the avocado, peaches and chicken and scatter over the mint. Serve with the potatoes while still warm.

Scotch broth

Ingredients

250g broth mix (or a mixture of 75g pearl barley, 75g yellow split peas, 50g red split lentils and 50g green split or marrowfat peas)

1 tbsp vegetable or olive oil

1 large onion, finely chopped

1 leek, washed and sliced

1 medium turnip, peeled and finely chopped

3 carrots, finely chopped

3 celery sticks, trimmed and finely chopped

3 litres lamb stock

200g kale chopped

Method

STEP 1

Rinse the soup mix and soak in cold water for 8 hrs or overnight, covered in a cool place. Drain and rinse well.

STEP 2

Heat the oil in a large pan and fry the onion, leek, turnip, carrots and celery for 10 mins, covered with a lid, until soft but not golden. Add a generous pinch of salt and a good grinding of pepper.

STEP 3

Pour the stock into the pan and bring to a simmer. Add the drained soup mix, and gently simmer for 1 hr part-covered, until the barley and split peas are tender. Season again if needed. Stir in the kale, and cook for 10-15 mins until tender, then ladle into bowls to serve.

Garlicky mushroom penne

Ingredients

210g can chickpeas, no need to drain

1 tbsp lemon juice

1 large garlic clove

1 tsp vegetable bouillon

2 tsp tahini

¼ tsp ground coriander

115g wholemeal penne

2 tsp rapeseed oil

2 red onions, halved and sliced

200g closed cup mushrooms, roughly chopped

½ lemon, juiced

generous handful chopped parsley

Method

STEP 1

To make the hummus, tip a 210g can chickpeas with the liquid into a bowl and add 1 tbsp lemon juice, 1 large garlic clove, 1 tsp vegetable bouillon, 2 tsp tahini and ¼ tsp ground coriander.

STEP 2

Blitz to a wet paste with a hand blender, still retaining some texture from the chickpeas.

STEP 3

Cook 115g wholemeal penne pasta according to the pack instructions.

STEP 4

Meanwhile, heat 2 tsp rapeseed oil in a non-stick wok or large frying pan and add 2 halved and sliced red onions and 200g roughly chopped closed cup mushrooms, stirring frequently until softened and starting to caramelise.

STEP 5

Toss together lightly, squeeze over the juice of ½ a lemon and serve, adding a dash of water to loosen the mixture a little if needed. Scatter with a generous handful of chopped parsley.

Falafel lunchbox

Ingredients

250g pouch cooked grains or lentils (we used red & white quinoa)

handful of baby spinach

¼ cucumber, chopped

handful of cherry tomatoes, halved

2 carrots, grated

1 pomegranate, seeds only

10 olives (optional)

12 falafel

4 tbsp hummus

drizzle of olive oil (optional)

½ lemon, quartered

Method

STEP 1

Divide the grains between the lunchboxes. Top each one with the vegetables, falafel, a spoonful of hummus and a drizzle of oil, if using, or divide the **Ingredients** between the compartments of a bento-style lunchbox. Put a lemon in each box for squeezing over just before eating.

Fish cakes with vegetables

Ingredients

450g firm white-fleshed fish such as cod or hoki

1 egg white

2 tsp cornflour

1 spring onion, finely chopped

1cm/½in fresh ginger, peeled and finely chopped

200ml/7fl oz peanut or vegetable oil, for frying

For the vegetables

8 dried cloud ear mushrooms (worth looking for, otherwise use dried shiitake)

1 tbsp finely chopped garlic

1cm/½in fresh ginger, peeled and finely sliced

1 small onion, cut into wedges

1 courgette, sliced into irregular chunks

half a cucumber, sliced into irregular chunks

1 onion squash, peeled and sliced into irregular chunks (optional)

3 tbsp chicken stock or water

For the sauce

3 tbsp oyster sauce

2 tsp light soy sauce

1 tsp golden caster sugar

1 tbsp rice wine

125ml chicken stock

1 tsp cornflour mixed with 1 tsp water

Method

STEP 1

Remove any skin from the fish fillets and then cut them into small pieces. Combine all the fish cake ingredients, except for the oil, in a food processor with 1 tsp of salt and 2 tbsp of water and blend the mixture until it's a firm paste.

STEP 2

Form the paste into two cakes, about 1cm thick. Heat the oil in a wok or large frying pan and fry each cake for 3-4 minutes on each side until golden. Remove with a slotted spoon and leave to drain and cool on paper towels.

STEP 3

While the fish cakes are cooling, soak the mushrooms in warm water for about 20 minutes until soft. Rinse well in cold water, drain, and set aside. When the fish cakes are cool, slice them into finger thick bite-size pieces.

STEP 4

Tip the oil out of the wok, leaving about 11/2 tbsp. Reheat the wok over a medium heat, add the garlic, ginger and onion wedges and stir fry for 1 minute. Add the courgette, cucumber, squash (if using), mushrooms and chicken stock and stir fry for another 2 minutes. Mix the sauce **Ingredients** together then pour into the stir fry and continue to cook for another 2 minutes or until the vegetables are cooked. Return the fish cake pieces to the pan and mix gently to heat through. Serve at once with boiled rice.

Spanish chicken traybake with chorizo & peppers

Ingredients

4 fat garlic cloves

1 tbsp fresh thyme leaves, plus a few sprigs

4 tsp olive oil

8 chicken thighs on the bone, excess skin trimmed

economy bag mixed peppers (about 700g), halved and deseeded

140g piece of chorizo, roughly chopped (we used a spicy one)

20 pitted black olives

200g cherry tomatoes

3 tbsp sherry vinegar or red wine vinegar

crusty bread, or keto bread, to serve

Method

STEP 1

Heat oven to 200C/180C fan/gas 6. Using a pestle and mortar, crush the garlic and thyme leaves with a little seasoning and 2 tsp oil to make a paste. If you don't have a pestle and mortar, finely grate the garlic, then stir everything together.

STEP 2

Rub the herb and garlic paste on the underside of the chicken to flavour it.

STEP 3

Cut each of the pepper halves into 2 or 3 chunky strips, depending on their size. Pile into a large roasting tin with the chorizo and olives, toss with the remaining oil, then sit the chicken on top, skin-side up. Scatter over the tomatoes, spoon over the vinegar, season and tuck in the thyme sprigs.

STEP 4

Roast for 1 hr until the chicken skin is crispy and the vegetables have softened. Serve with crusty or keto bread, pasta or potatoes.

Bulgur & quinoa lunch bowls

Ingredients

For the bulgur base

1 large onion, very finely chopped

150g bulgur and quinoa (this comes ready mixed)

2sprigs of thyme

2 tsp vegetable bouillon powder

For the avocado topping

1 avocado, halved, destoned and chopped

2 tomatoes, cut into wedges

4 tbsp chopped basil

6 Kalamata olives, halved

2 tsp extra virgin olive oil

2 tsp cider vinegar

2 big handfuls of rocket

For the beetroot topping

210g can chickpeas, drained

160g cooked beetroot, diced

2 tomatoes, cut into wedges

2 tbsp chopped mint

1 tsp cumin seeds

several pinches of ground cinnamon

2 tsp extra virgin olive oil

2 tsp cider vinegar

1 orange, cut into segments

2 tbsp toasted pine nuts

Method

STEP 1

Tip the onion and bulgur mix into a pan, pour over 600ml water and stir in the thyme and bouillon. Cook, covered, over a low heat for 15 mins, then leave to stand for 10 mins. All the liquid should now be absorbed. When cool, remove the thyme and divide the bulgur between four bowls or plastic containers.

STEP 2

For the avocado topping, toss all the **Ingredients** together except for the rocket. Pile onto two portions of the bulgur and top with the rocket.

STEP 3

For the beetroot topping, first pile the chickpeas on top, then toss the beetroot with the tomato, mint, cumin, a good pinch of cinnamon, the oil and vinegar. Toss well, add the orange, then pile onto the remaining portions of bulghur, scatter with the pine nuts and sprinkle with extra cinnamon. Chill in the fridge until needed.

Roasted roots & sage soup

Ingredients

1 parsnip, peeled and chopped

2 carrots, peeled and chopped

300g turnip, swede or celeriac, chopped

4 garlic cloves, skin left on

1 tbsp rapeseed oil, plus ½ tsp

1 tsp maple syrup

¼ small bunch of sage, leaves picked, 4 whole, the rest finely chopped

750ml vegetable stock

grating of nutmeg

1½ tbsp fat-free yogurt

Method

STEP 1

Heat the oven to 200C/180C fan/gas 6. Toss the root vegetables and garlic with 1 tbsp oil and season. Tip onto a baking tray and roast for 30 mins until tender. Toss with the maple syrup and the chopped sage, then roast for another 10 mins until golden and glazed. Brush the whole sage leaves with ½ tsp oil and add to the baking tray in the last 3-4 mins to crisp up, then remove and set aside.

STEP 2

Scrape the vegetables into a pan, squeeze the garlic out of the skins, discarding the papery shells, and add with the stock, then blend with a stick blender until very smooth and creamy. Bring to a simmer and season with salt, pepper and nutmeg.

STEP 3

Divide between bowls. Serve with a swirl of yogurt and the crispy sage leaves.

Tempeh traybake

Ingredients

200g pack organic unflavoured tempeh, thickly sliced

1 red pepper, deseeded and cut into small chunks

1 red onion, cut into wedges

160g sweet potatoes, cut into wedges

200g baby potatoes, halved

130g whole baby corn

1 courgette (160g), thickly sliced

2 tsp olive or rapeseed oil

1 tsp dried oregano

1⁄2 lemon, juiced

2-3 tbsp thyme leaves

For the marinade

1 tbsp tomato purée

1 tsp smoked paprika

2 tsp balsamic vinegar

2 garlic cloves, finely grated

10g finely chopped dates

2 tsp olive or rapeseed oil

Method

STEP 1

Heat the oven to 190C/170C fan/gas 5. Mix the marinade **Ingredients** with plenty of black pepper and 2 tbsp water in a bowl, then stir in the tempeh to coat it. Set aside for 15 mins to marinate.

STEP 2

Pile the vegetables onto a large baking tray and toss with the oil and oregano. Bake for 10 mins, then add the tempeh along with any remaining marinade, and bake for 30 mins more until the veg is tender. Leave to cool a little, then squeeze over the lemon juice to taste (start with a quarter) and scatter over the fresh thyme.

Toasted quinoa, lentil & poached salmon salad

Ingredients

140g quinoa

1 tsp olive oil

400ml light vegetable stock (we used bouillon)

250g asparagus, trimmed

100g frozen soya bean

140g broccoli, florets trimmed and halved (we used Tenderstem)

zest and juice 1 lemon

2 salmon fillets (about 150g each)

½ garlic clove, crushed

250g pack ready-cooked puy lentils

6 spring onions, sliced on the diagonal

large handful mint and parsley, roughly chopped

85g baby spinach leaves

25g flaked almond, toasted

Method

STEP 1

Rinse the quinoa and tip into a large non-stick frying pan. Turn the heat to medium and dry out the grains, stirring to move them about the pan. Once all the liquid has evaporated, stir in the oil. Continue cooking the quinoa until it has turned a nutty brown and starts to 'pop' – this will take 10-15 mins. Stir every so often to stop the quinoa burning. Pour over the stock and simmer for 15-20 mins until all the liquid has been absorbed. Tip into a bowl and allow to cool.

STEP 2

Meanwhile, bring a large pan of water to the boil. Drop in the soya beans, asparagus and broccoli, and simmer for 2 mins. Remove using a slotted spoon and plunge into a bowl of ice-cold water. Drain the vegetables.

STEP 3

Add 1 tsp of the lemon juice to the pan with the vegetable water, then turn the heat down to a gentle simmer. Season the salmon fillets and submerge fully in the water. Poach for 6-8 mins until just cooked. Remove, allow to cool, then take off the skin and flake into large chunks.

STEP 4

Make a dressing by mixing together the garlic, most of the lemon zest and remaining lemon juice. Mix the quinoa, lentils, drained vegetables, spring onions, herbs, spinach and dressing together in a large bowl, then season. Pile onto a serving plate, top with the salmon, then scatter over the almonds and remaining lemon zest.

Malt loaf

Ingredients

sunflower oil, for greasing

150ml hot black tea

175g malt extract, plus extra for glazing (see tip)

85g dark muscovado sugar

300g mixed dried fruit

2 large eggs, beaten

250g plain flour

1 tsp baking powder

½ tsp bicarbonate of soda

Method

STEP 1

Heat oven to 150C/130C fan/gas 2. Line the base and ends of two greased 450g/1lb non-stick loaf tins with strips of baking parchment.

STEP 2

Pour the hot tea into a mixing bowl with the malt, sugar and dried fruit. Stir well, then add the eggs.

STEP 3

Tip in the flour, then quickly stir in the baking powder and bicarbonate of soda and pour into the prepared tins. Bake for 50 mins until firm and well risen. While still warm, brush with a little more malt to glaze and leave to cool.

STEP 4

Remove from the tins. If you can bear not to eat it straight away, it gets more sticky after wrapping and keeping for 2-5 days. Serve sliced and buttered, if you like.

DINNER RECIPES FOR WEIGHT LOSS

Fragrant vegetable & cashew biryani

Ingredients

500g basmati rice

2 large onions, halved and thinly sliced

4 tbsp sunflower oil

thumb-size piece fresh root ginger, shredded

65g sachet korma curry paste (we used Sharwood's)

2 cinnamon sticks

6 green cardamom pods

3 star anise

250g diced potatoes

1 small cauliflower, cut into small florets

250g Greek yogurt

225g frozen peas

2 good pinches saffron

½ tsp rosewater

butter, for greasing

100g roasted, salted cashew nuts

For the garnish

2 onions, halved and very thinly sliced

3 tbsp sunflower oil

good handful coriander

Method

STEP 1

Rinse the rice in several changes of water to remove excess starch, then put in a bowl of cold water and leave to soak for 30 mins.

STEP 2

Meanwhile, fry the onions in the oil for 8 mins until soft and starting to colour. Add the ginger, then cook for 2 mins more. Stir in the curry paste followed by the whole spices, cook for 1 min more, then tip in the potatoes and cauliflower. Pour in 300ml water, cover and boil for about 5-7 mins until the veg are just tender, but still have a little resistance. Stir in the yogurt and peas with 1 tsp salt.

STEP 3

Mix the saffron, rosewater and 3 tbsp boiling water together and stir well. Drain the rice, tip into a pan of boiling salted water, then cook for 5 mins until almost tender. Drain again. Get out a large ovenproof dish with a lid and butter the base. Tip the curry sauce into the base, scatter over the nuts, then spoon over the rice. Drizzle over the rosewater mixture, then cover with foil followed by the lid. Can be chilled overnight until ready to cook.

STEP 4

Heat oven to 180C/fan 160C/gas 4. Put the biryani in the oven for 45 mins-1 hr until thoroughly heated through. To check it's ready, try a spoonful from the centre of the rice. For the garnish, slowly fry the onions in the oil until really golden and crisp (this can be done in advance). When the biryani is hot and ready to serve, gently toss through the onions and coriander.

Spiced vegetable pilaf

Ingredients

6 carrots, cut lengthways into 6-8 wedges

3 red onions, cut into wedges

2 tbsp olive oil

2 tsp cumin seeds

4 cardamom pods

1 cinnamon stick

200g brown basmati rice, rinsed

400ml vegetable stock

400g can brown lentils, rinsed and drained

200g baby spinach

handful toasted flaked almonds, or a few whole almonds (optional)

Method

STEP 1

Heat oven to 200C/180C fan/gas 6. In boiling water, cook carrots for 4 mins, tipping in onions for the last min of cooking. Drain and mix in a roasting tin with 4 tsp oil, the cumin and seasoning. Roast for 30 mins, while you cook the rice.

STEP 2

Heat remaining 2 tsp oil in a large pan. Add cardamom and cinnamon for 30 secs, then add rice and toast for 1 min. Pour over stock and 100ml water, then simmer, covered, for 25-30 mins, until rice is tender and the water absorbed. Remove cinnamon and cardamom.

STEP 3

Tip in lentils and fork through before topping with spinach. Put lid back on and cook over a low heat, stirring once, until spinach has wilted and lentils heated through. Fork through again before tipping the cumin roasted veg onto the top and sprinkling with almonds, if using.

Broccoli & stilton soup

Ingredients

2 tbsp rapeseed oil

1 onion, finely chopped

1 stick celery, sliced

1 leek, sliced

1 medium potato, diced

1 knob butter

1l low salt or homemade chicken or vegetable stock

1 head broccoli, roughly chopped

140g stilton, or other blue cheese, crumbled

Method

STEP 1

Heat 2 tbsp rapeseed oil in a large saucepan and then add 1 finely chopped onion. Cook on a medium heat until soft. Add a splash of water if the onion starts to catch.

STEP 2

Add 1 sliced celery stick, 1 sliced leek, 1 diced medium potato and a knob of butter. Stir until melted, then cover with a lid. Allow to sweat for 5 minutes then remove the lid.

STEP 3

Pour in 1l of chicken or vegetable stock and add any chunky bits of stalk from 1 head of broccoli. Cook for 10-15 minutes until all the vegetables are soft.

STEP 4

Add the rest of the roughly chopped broccoli and cook for a further 5 minutes.

STEP 5

Carefully transfer to a blender and blitz until smooth.

STEP 6

Stir in 140g crumbled stilton, allowing a few lumps to remain. Season with black pepper and serve.

Mango & passion fruit fool

Ingredients

2 large ripe mangoes

4 passion fruits, halved

2 x 150g/5oz tubs Greek yogurt (use low-fat if you prefer)

juice 1 lime

Method

STEP 1

Peel the mangoes using a vegetable peeler. Slice the cheeks off one and cut into small dice. Set aside.

STEP 2

Cut the flesh from the remaining mango and stone, then purée flesh in a liquidiser. Squeeze out the seeds from 2 of the passion fruit halves and mix with the mango purée. Add lime juice to taste. Gently fold the yogurt and half the diced mango through the fruity purée.

STEP 3

Divide between 4 glasses and top with the remaining diced mango. Cover and chill for 30 mins before eating. Scoop the seeds from the remaining passion fruit over the top of the fools to serve.

Warm grain salad with bacon, leeks & spinach

Ingredients

200g farro or quinoa

1l vegetable, pork or chicken stock

4 rashers smoked pancetta or streaky bacon

1 leek

knob of salted butter

4 tbsp extra virgin olive oil

1 rosemary sprig, leaves only

2 large handfuls of baby spinach leaves, washed, or shredded kale

100g chestnuts, cooked and broken up (optional)

Method

STEP 1

Boil the farro or quinoa in the stock in a lidded pan until soft to the bite, then drain. Meanwhile, use a pair of scissors to cut the bacon into small strips. Wash the leek and chop finely. Melt the butter with the oil and fry the bacon, leeks and rosemary gently over a medium heat until soft.

STEP 2

Add the farro to the pan, and stir in the green leaves and chestnuts, if you like. Put the lid on the pan and keep over a low heat until the leaves wilt and the chestnuts warm through. Serve warm or at room temperature

Carrot & coriander soup

Ingredients

1 tbsp vegetable oil

1 onion, chopped

1 tsp ground coriander

1 potato, chopped

450g carrots, peeled and chopped

1.2l vegetable or chicken stock

handful coriander (about ½ a supermarket packet)

Method

STEP 1

Heat 1 tbsp vegetable oil in a large pan, add 1 chopped onion, then fry for 5 mins until softened.

STEP 2

Stir in 1 tsp ground coriander and 1 chopped potato, then cook for 1 min.

STEP 3

Add the 450g peeled and chopped carrots and 1.2l vegetable or chicken stock, bring to the boil, then reduce the heat.

STEP 4

Cover and cook for 20 mins until the carrots are tender.

STEP 5

Tip into a food processor with a handful of coriander then blitz until smooth (you may need to do this in two batches). Return to pan, taste, add salt if necessary, then reheat to serve.

Fridge-raid fried rice

Ingredients

2 tbsp vegetable oil

1 white onion, finely chopped

1 carrot, finely chopped

100g green beans, chopped

1 red or yellow pepper, finely chopped

½ medium broccoli, chopped into small florets

150g cooked chicken (or any other meat), roughly chopped, optional

300g cold cooked rice

2 eggs, beaten

1 tbsp sesame oil

1 tbsp oyster sauce

1 spring onion, finely sliced

1 tsp toasted sesame seeds

Method

STEP 1

Heat half the vegetable oil in a wok or a frying pan over a medium-high heat, and stir-fry the onions, carrots and green beans for 5 mins. Add the peppers, broccoli and chicken, and stir-fry for 3 mins more.

STEP 2

Tip in the rice and stir-fry for another 4 mins until all the grains of rice have separated. Push the rice and vegetables to the side, then add the remaining vegetable oil to the other. Crack in the egg and scramble briefly before stirring into the veg and chicken mixture.

STEP 3

Stir in the sesame oil and oyster sauce to coat, then garnish with the spring onions and sesame seeds.

Pineapple & passion fruit cheesecake

Ingredients

For the base

10 digestive biscuits

6 ginger nut biscuits

For the filling

2 x 300g tubs full-fat soft cheese

3 large eggs, beaten

142ml pot double cream

140g caster sugar

zest 3 limes

For the topping

medium, ripe pineapple, peeled, cored and quartered

3 ripe passion fruits, halved

284g pot double cream

1 tbsp icing sugar

Method

STEP 1

Heat oven to 160C/fan 140C/gas 2. Put the biscuits into a plastic bag, seal tightly and bash with a rolling pin until you have fine crumbs. Tip into a bowl and mix in the melted butter. Spoon the crumbs into the base of a 23cm springform tin and press down with the back of a spoon. Bake for 10-15 mins until lightly browned, then cool.

STEP 2

Put all of the filling **Ingredients** in a large bowl and beat until smooth. Pour onto the cooled biscuit base and return to the oven for 50 mins to 1 hr until the filling is just set and starting to brown. Leave the cheesecake to cool in the oven with the door slightly open, then chill in the fridge. If the top has cracked it doesn't matter. Can be made up to 2 days ahead. Carefully remove from tin and transfer onto a serving plate.

STEP 3

Slice the pineapple quarters lengthways as thinly as you can. Whip the cream and icing sugar until thickened, but not stiff. Spread over the top of the cheesecake, then pile the pineapple on top. Scoop the pulp and seeds of the passion fruit over the top.

Roasted sweet potato & carrot soup

Ingredients

500g sweet potatoes, peeled and cut into chunks

300g carrots, peeled and cut into chunks

3 tbsp olive oil

2 onions, finely chopped

2 garlic cloves, crushed

1l vegetable stock

100ml crème fraîche, plus extra to serve

Method

STEP 1

Heat oven to 220C/200C fan/ gas 7 and put 500g chunked sweet potatoes and 300g chunked carrots into a large roasting tin, drizzled with 2 tbsp olive oil and plenty of seasoning.

STEP 2

Roast the vegetables in the oven for 25-30 mins or until caramelised and tender.

STEP 3

Meanwhile, put the remaining 1 tbsp olive oil in a large deep saucepan and fry 2 finely chopped onions over a medium-low heat for about 10 mins until softened.

STEP 4

Add 2 crushed garlic cloves and stir for 1 min before adding 1l vegetable stock. Simmer for 5-10 mins until the onions are very soft, then set aside.

STEP 5

Once the roasted vegetables are done, leave to cool a little, then transfer to the saucepan and use a hand blender to process until smooth. Stir in 100ml crème fraîche, a little more seasoning and reheat until hot.

STEP 6

Serve in bowls topped with a swirl of crème fraîche and a good grinding of black pepper.

Cottage pie

Ingredients

3 tbsp olive oil

1¼kg beef mince

2 onions, finely chopped

3 carrots, chopped

3 celery sticks, chopped

2 garlic cloves, finely chopped

3 tbsp plain flour

1 tbsp tomato purée

large glass of red wine (optional)

850ml beef stock

4 tbsp Worcestershire sauce

a few thyme sprigs

2 bay leaves

For the mash

1.8kg potatoes, chopped

225ml milk

25g butter

200g strong cheddar, grated

freshly grated nutmeg

Method

STEP 1

Heat 1 tbsp olive oil in a large saucepan and fry 1¼kg beef mince until browned – you may need to do this in batches. Set aside as it browns.

STEP 2

Put the other 2 tbsp olive oil into the pan, add 2 finely chopped onions, 3 chopped carrots and 3 chopped celery sticks and cook on a gentle heat until soft, about 20 mins.

STEP 3

Add 2 finely chopped garlic cloves, 3 tbsp plain flour and 1 tbsp tomato purée, increase the heat and cook for a few mins, then return the beef to the pan.

STEP 4

Pour over a large glass of red wine, if using, and boil to reduce it slightly before adding the 850ml beef stock, 4 tbsp Worcestershire sauce, a few thyme sprigs and 2 bay leaves.

STEP 5

Bring to a simmer and cook, uncovered, for 45 mins. By this time the gravy should be thick and coating the meat. Check after about 30 mins – if a lot of liquid remains, increase the heat slightly to reduce the gravy a little. Season well, then discard the bay leaves and thyme stalks.

STEP 6

Meanwhile, make the mash. In a large saucepan, cover the 1.8kg potatoes which you've peeled and chopped, in salted cold water, bring to the boil and simmer until tender.

STEP 7

Drain well, then allow to steam-dry for a few mins. Mash well with the 225ml milk, 25g butter, and three-quarters of the 200g strong cheddar cheese, then season with freshly grated nutmeg and some salt and pepper.

STEP 8

Spoon the meat into 2 ovenproof dishes. Pipe or spoon on the mash to cover. Sprinkle on the remaining cheese.

STEP 9

If eating straight away, heat oven to 220C/200C fan/gas 7 and cook for 25-30 mins, or until the topping is golden.

STEP 10

If you want to use a slow cooker, brown your mince in batches then tip into your slow cooker and stir in the vegetables, flour, purée, wine, stock, Worcestershire sauce and herbs with some seasoning. Cover and cook on High for 4-5 hours. Make the mash following the previous steps, and then oven cook in the same way to finish.

Coriander chicken with rice & spiced vegetables

Ingredients

For the coriander chutney

50g coriander (about 2 small packs)

50g unsalted peanuts

½ lemon, juiced

1 green chilli, deseeded and finely chopped

2 tsp garam masala

½ tsp soft brown sugar

For the chicken

2 tbsp vegetable oil

2 onions, sliced

thumb-sized piece ginger, finely grated

4 garlic cloves, crushed

1 green chilli, finely chopped

6 skinless and boneless chicken thigh fillets, cut into 3cm chunks

For the rice

350g basmati rice

1 tbsp coconut oil

½ tsp chilli flakes

2cm piece ginger, finely grated

For the spiced vegetables

125g pack purple sprouting broccoli or long-stemmed broccoli

200g fine green beans

1 tsp oil

2cm piece ginger, sliced

¼ tsp chilli flakes

Method

STEP 1

Use a stick blender or mini food processor to whizz up all the chutney ingredients, then chill.

STEP 2

Heat the oil in a large, lidded frying pan over a medium-high heat. Add the onions and fry for 9-10 mins, then add the ginger, garlic and chilli. Cook for a few mins more, then add the chicken.

Brown well, then add half the coriander chutney and reduce the heat. Cover and cook for 15-20 mins or until the chicken is cooked through.

STEP 3

Rinse the rice in a sieve, then tip into a large, lidded saucepan. Stir in all the **Ingredients** for the rice. Pour over enough boiling water to cover the rice by 1cm, cover, bring to the boil and cook for 5 mins. Turn off the heat and leave to steam-cook with the lid on for 20 mins. Fluff up with a fork, then season.

STEP 4

Put the broccoli and green beans in a pan and add 100ml boiling water. Cover and cook over a medium-high heat for 4-5 mins. Drain and return to the pan with the oil, ginger, chilli flakes and some seasoning. Cook for another 2 mins, then serve with the chicken, remaining chutney and the rice.

Roasted stone fruits

Ingredients

3 peaches, halved, stoned and cut in chunky wedges

3 nectarines, halved, stoned and cut in chunky wedges

6 apricots, halved and stoned

400ml marsala

2 tbsp honey

50g butter

Method

STEP 1

Heat oven to 180C/160C fan/gas 4. Toss all the fruits into a snug ovenproof dish or roasting tin. Pour over the Marsala, drizzle over the honey and dot with the butter. Roast for 30 mins until the fruits are juicy and tender but not mushy. Serve warm with their juices, scoops of ice cream and florentines

Vegetable couscous with chickpeas & preserved lemons

Ingredients

For the broth

2l vegetable or chicken stock

3 tbsp harissa, homemade (see recipe below) or shop bought

3 carrots, chopped

3 large parsnips, chopped

2 red onions, cut into wedges through the root

2 large potatoes, chopped into chunks

½ butternut squash, chopped into chunks

4 leeks, sliced into rings

12 dried figs, halved

2 preserved lemons, homemade (see recipe below) or bought, rinsed, pulp scooped out and finely sliced

small bunch mint, chopped

For the couscous

200g couscous

400g can chickpea

25g butter

1 red onion, finely diced

3 spring onions, sliced

2 tbsp harissa

50ml olive oil

juice 1 lemon

bunch coriander, roughly chopped

Method

STEP 1

For the broth, bring the stock to a simmer in a large pan. Add the harissa and vegetables, bring back to the boil, then reduce heat and simmer for 15 mins. Add the figs and continue to cook for 5 mins more until the veg is tender.

STEP 2

Meanwhile, put the couscous and half the chickpeas into a bowl, add the butter, and season. Pour 350ml boiling water over the couscous, cover with cling film, leave aside for 10 mins, then fluff up with a fork.

STEP 3

In a separate bowl, combine the red onion, spring onions, harissa, olive oil, remaining chickpeas, lemon juice and coriander, then mix into the couscous. Pile onto a large deep serving dish, ladle over the braised vegetables and broth, and sprinkle with the preserved lemons and chopped mint.

Chilli coconut pork with vegetable noodle salad

Ingredients

2 tsp sunflower oil

1 pork fillet, weighing about 400g/14oz, sliced into finger-thick strips

1 tbsp Madras curry paste

2 tbsp crunchy peanut butter

200ml carton coconut cream

300ml vegetable stock

200g medium or thin noodle

2 x 200g bags washed and ready-to-cook vegetable medley (we used beans, broccoli, carrot and baby corn mix)

3 tbsp sweet chilli dipping sauce

zest and juice 1 lime

Method

STEP 1

Heat the oil in a wok until really hot. Add the pork and stir fry for 2 minutes until lightly browned. Stir in the curry paste and cook for 1 minute until fragrant, then stir in the peanut butter. Pour over the coconut cream and stock and bring to the boil. Simmer for 7 minutes, stirring occasionally until you have a thickish sauce and the pork is cooked.

STEP 2

While the pork is simmering, cook the noodles according to the pack instructions. Cook the vegetables in the microwave as per the pack instructions.

STEP 3

Drain the noodles. Return the noodles to a bowl and toss in the cooked vegetables and sweet chilli dipping sauce. Stir the lime zest and juice in with the pork and season to taste. Ladle the pork and noodle salad into four serving bowls.

Fish gratin with vegetables & prawns

Ingredients

softened butter, for the dish

150g long-grain rice

100g carrots, cut into 1cm cubes (or use canned or frozen carrots)

100g leeks, sliced into ½cm-thick rounds

400g white skinless fish fillets (haddock or seabass work well)

150g cooked prawns

2 eggs, separated

75g mayonnaise

75g crème fraîche

150g cheddar, grated

Method

STEP 1

Heat the oven to 180C/160C fan/ gas 4 and butter an ovenproof baking dish (ours was 4cm deep). Cook the rice in a pan of lightly salted boiling water for 12 mins until tender, then drain and tip into the base of the prepared dish.

STEP 2

Cook the carrots in a pan of boiling water for 10-12 mins until just tender, or tip into a heatproof bowl with a splash of water and microwave for 2-3 mins. (If you're using canned or frozen carrots, you can skip this.) Mix the carrots with the leeks and spoon this over the rice, spreading it out to cover.

STEP 3

To prepare the fish, remove the skin and any pin bones, then cut it into pieces. Arrange the fish over the vegetables, then scatter over the prawns.

STEP 4

Mix the egg yolks, mayo, crème fraîche and cheese together, and season.

STEP 5

Tip the egg whites into a clean bowl and beat with an electric whisk to stiff peaks. Gently fold the whipped egg whites into the mayonnaise mixture, then spoon this over the layer of fish and prawns in the dish. Spread it out with a spatula or the back of the spoon so it completely covers the fish. Bake for 20-25 mins, or until the topping is lightly golden brown. Leave to stand for a few minutes, then serve straight from the dish.

Chargrilled vegetable salad

Ingredients

2 red peppers

3 tbsp olive oil

1 tbsp red wine vinegar

1 small garlic clove, crushed

1 red chilli, deseeded, finely chopped

1 aubergine, cut into 1cm rounds

2 red onions, sliced about 1.5cm thick but kept as whole slices

6 plump sundried tomatoes in oil, drained and torn into strips

handful black olives

large handful basil, roughly torn

Method

STEP 1

First, blacken the peppers all over – do this directly over a flame, over hot coals or under a hot grill.

When completely blackened, put them in a bowl, cover with a plate and leave to cool.

STEP 2

While the peppers are cooling, mix the oil, vinegar, garlic and chilli in a large bowl. On a hot barbecue or griddle pan, chargrill the aubergine, courgette and onions in batches until they have defined grill marks on both sides and are starting to soften. The time will depend on the intensity of your grill, so use your judgement – courgettes and red onions are fine still slightly crunchy but you want the aubergine cooked all the way through. As the vegetables are ready, put them straight into the dressing to marinate, breaking the onions up into rings.

STEP 3

When the peppers are cool enough to handle, peel, remove the stalk and scrape out the seeds. Cut into strips and toss through the veg with any juice from the bowl. Mix in the tomatoes, olives, basil and seasoning. Drizzle with more oil, if you like, and serve either on its own or with mozzarella or crumbled feta.

Spring vegetable noodles

Ingredients

2 tbsp olive oil

3 smoked back bacon rashers

250g green vegetables eg asparagus and broccoli,
cut into bite-sized pieces

2 garlic cloves, finely sliced

6 spring onions, trimmed, halved lengthways and
quartered

150g pack Amoy Straight to Wok new noodle

soy sauce, to serve

Method

STEP 1

Heat the oil in a wok. Using scissors, snip the bacon into the hot oil and fry, stirring occasionally, for 2 minutes.

STEP 2

Tip the asparagus and broccoli into the wok with the garlic and spring onions. Stir fry for about a minute then top with the noodles and petits pois and drizzle over a tablespoon of water. Cover the pan and let everything steam for 4 minutes until the broccoli is just tender.

STEP 3

Mix everything together and serve straight away, with a bottle of soy sauce on the table so each person can add their own, according to taste.

Roast chicken risotto with chicken crackling

Ingredients

1 leftover roast chicken carcass (you'll need about 300-400g meat, and as much skin as you can get from the carcass)

1 carrot, halved lengthways

2 onions, 1 unpeeled and halved, 1 peeled and finely chopped

2 bay leaves

2 chicken stock cubes

25g butter, plus a large knob

2 tbsp olive oil

3 large garlic cloves, crushed

300g risotto rice

125ml white wine

½ lemon, zested

small bunch of thyme, leaves picked

50g grated parmesan, plus extra shavings to serve

truffle oil or extra virgin olive oil, for drizzling

Method

STEP 1

Strip all the meat from the chicken carcass, shredding it into bite-sized pieces. Transfer to a plate along with any skin you can salvage and any jellied juices and fat, then chill until needed. Put the carcass in a large saucepan with the carrot, halved onion and bay leaves. Cover with cold water, then bring to the boil. Reduce the heat to a gentle simmer, cover and cook for at least 30 mins and up to 2 hrs until you have about 1 litre of stock. Strain through a sieve into a large jug or pan. Discard the bones, bay and veg. If you end up with more than 1 litre of stock, continue to cook over a high heat to reduce. Whisk in the stock cubes until dissolved, then keep the pan warm over a low heat while you make the risotto.

STEP 2

Heat a large casserole or high- sided frying pan over a low heat. Melt the butter, add the oil and fry the chopped onion for 10 mins until soft and translucent. Add the garlic and stir for 1 min more, then add the rice. Cook, continuing to stir for a few minutes until the rice has absorbed some of the butter and is shiny. Pour in the wine and stir until the liquid has bubbled away.

STEP 3

Add the lemon zest and thyme, then a generous ladleful of the warm stock. Continue to cook the risotto over a low-medium heat for 20 mins, stirring often, adding the stock a ladleful at a time and allowing it to be absorbed before the next addition. Add the reserved chicken and any jellied juices and fat towards the end of the cooking time to warm through. The risotto should be loose and soupy, and the rice grains very nearly cooked, but still retaining a little bite. Stir in some more stock to loosen if needed (or kettle-hot water if you've run out), then a large knob of butter and the parmesan. Season well and cover. Leave for a few minutes for the butter and cheese to be absorbed while you make the crackling.

STEP 4

Tear or chop the chicken skin into small pieces, then put in a cold, dry frying pan. If the skin is quite lean (with no fatty patches) add a drizzle of oil; otherwise, the fat should render from the skin and start to sizzle. Fry for a few minutes until the skin is crisp, then transfer to a plate lined with kitchen paper.

STEP 5

Check the consistency of the risotto again – the rice will absorb more stock as it rests, so you may need to add more. Spoon into bowls, drizzle with truffle or olive oil, and top with some shaved parmesan and the chicken crackling.

Chicken & vegetable stew with wholemeal couscous

Ingredients

1 tbsp olive oil

2 skinless chicken breasts, cut into chunks

1 small onion, sliced

1 garlic clove, crushed

pinch each paprika and saffron

50g baby sweetcorn, halved

50g asparagus tips

50g peas

50g cherry tomatoes, halved

150ml chicken stock

140g wholemeal couscous

Method

STEP 1

Heat the oil in a pan, cook the chicken for 5-6 mins, then remove with a slotted spoon. Add onion and cook for 2-3 mins before adding the garlic, paprika, saffron, sweetcorn, asparagus, peas and tomatoes. Cook for 2-3 mins more. Return the chicken to the pan, pour in the stock, then cover and simmer for 15 mins.

STEP 2

Meanwhile, cook the couscous following pack instructions. To serve, fluff the couscous with a fork and divide between 2 bowls before spooning over the stew.

Layered roast summer vegetables

Ingredients

6 tbsp good-quality olive oil

4 large courgettes, thickly sliced (yellow ones look pretty)

5 ripe plum tomatoes, sliced

2 aubergines, sliced

1 large garlic bulb, kept whole

small bunch rosemary, broken into sprigs

Method

STEP 1

Heat oven to 220C/200C fan/gas 7. Drizzle a round ovenproof dish with a little oil; then, starting from the outside, tightly layer alternate slices of the vegetables in concentric circles until you get to the middle – sit the head of garlic here. If you have any vegetables left, tuck them into any gaps around the outside. Stick the sprigs of rosemary among the vegetables, drizzle everything generously with olive oil, then season with salt and pepper.

STEP 2

Roast everything together, drizzling with more oil occasionally, for 50 mins-1 hr, until the vegetables are soft and lightly charred.

STEP 3

Remove from the oven and leave to stand for a few mins, then remove the garlic and separate it into cloves for squeezing over the vegetables.

Roast vegetable cassoulet

Ingredients

350g dried haricot beans

a bundle of thyme, bay leaf and parsley stalks

3 medium onions, 1 quartered, 2 chopped

450g carrots, 2 quartered, rest in chunks

11 tbsp extra-virgin olive oil

2 celery sticks, chopped

4 garlic cloves, chopped

400g can chopped tomatoes

1 tsp light muscovado sugar

4 tsp chopped fresh tarragon

1 medium butternut squash, peeled, seeded and cut into chunks

1 medium celeriac, peeled and cut into chunks

1 tbsp Dijon mustard

4 tbsp chopped fresh parsley

85g fresh white bread crumbs

Method

STEP 1

Bring the beans to boil in a saucepan of cold water, simmer for 5 minutes, take off heat and cover tightly. Leave for 2 hours.

STEP 2

Drain the beans, return to pan, cover with fresh cold water and add the herb bundle and vegetable quarters. Bring to boil and simmer for 1 hour until tender.

STEP 3

Preheat oven to 200C/Gas 6/fan oven 180C. Heat 3 tablespoons of the oil in a casserole and fry the chopped onion and celery until soft. Add the garlic and cook for 3-4 minutes. Stir in the tomatoes, sugar and half the tarragon. Season.

STEP 4

Drain beans, retaining 1.2 litres/2 pints of liquid. Discard veg and herbs. Stir 600ml/1 pint of the liquid into the tomato mixture and simmer, half-covered, for 30 minutes. Toss the squash, carrot and celeriac chunks in 5 tablespoons of oil. Season and roast in a tray for 30 minutes.

STEP 5

Remove vegetables and reduce heat to 180C/Gas 4/fan oven 160C. Stir beans, vegetables, mustard and half the parsley into the casserole. Add liquid if needed to make the mixture nicely moist. Check seasoning. Turn into a wide baking dish. (You can prepare to this stage the day before. Cool, cover and refrigerate. Next day, if the beans have absorbed too much liquid, moisten with bean liquid or stock.)

STEP 6

Mix the breadcrumbs with the remaining parsley and tarragon. Scatter over and drizzle with remaining oil. Bake for 50 minutes. (Add an extra 10 minutes if making ahead.) Serve from the dish.

SNACKS RECIPES FOR WEIGHT LOSS

Carrot cake fridge flapjacks

Ingredients

170g butter, chopped, plus extra for the tin

200g pitted dates, roughly chopped

250g honey

2 large carrots, coarsely grated

300g rolled oats

100g dried cranberries

150g dried apricots, chopped

70g chopped walnuts

70g mixed seeds

2 tsp mixed spice

2 tsp ground cinnamon

For the icing

1 tbsp soft cheese

2 tbsp icing sugar, sieved

1 small orange, zested, plus 1-2 tbsp orange juice

Method

STEP 1

Boil the kettle. Heat the oven to 170C/150C fan/gas 3½, butter a 20 x 30cm cake tin and line with baking parchment. Tip the dates into a heatproof bowl and cover with 60ml boiling water from the kettle. Set aside to rehydrate for 10 mins, then tip into a food processor and blitz until smooth.

STEP 2

Melt the butter and honey in a saucepan over a low heat, stirring until smooth. Tip the carrots, oats, cranberries, apricots, chopped walnuts, mixed seeds, mixed spice, cinnamon and a small pinch of salt into a large bowl. Stir the sweetened butter and puréed dates into the dry **Ingredients** until combined, then tip into the prepared tin and press into an even layer using a spatula. Bake for 45-50 mins, covering with foil halfway through if the flapjacks brown too quickly. Cool in the tin. Once completely cool, chill in the fridge for at least 3 hrs.

STEP 3

For the icing, whisk all of the **Ingredients** together until smooth. Drizzle the icing over the flapjacks and cut into 12 bars. Will keep, covered in the fridge, for three days.

Raspberry & pine nut bars

Ingredients

200g plain flour

200g porridge oat

250g pack butter, room temperature, cut into small pieces

175g light muscovado sugar

finely grated zest of 1 lemon

100g pack pine nut

2 punnets raspberries (total weight 250g/9oz)

Method

STEP 1

Preheat the oven to fan 170C/ conventional 190C/gas 5. Butter a shallow 23cm square tin. Tip the flour, oats and butter into a mixing bowl and use your fingers to work the mixture together to make coarse crumbs. Mix in the sugar, lemon zest and three quarters of the pine nuts using your hands, then press the mixture together well so it forms large sticky clumps.

STEP 2

Drop about two thirds of the oat mixture into the base of the tin, spread it out and press down very lightly – don't pack it too firmly. Scatter the raspberries on top, sprinkle the rest of the oat mixture over, then the rest of the pine nuts and press everything down lightly.

STEP 3

Bake for 35-40 minutes until pale golden on top. Cut into 12 bars with a sharp knife while still warm, then leave to cool in the tin before removing. Will keep for 2-3 days.

Rice paper rolls

Ingredients

50g rice vermicelli noodles

1 carrot, peeled

1 avocado, peeled and destoned

¼ cucumber

8 rice paper wraps

8 king prawns, peeled and cooked

8 mint leaves

½ cooked chicken breast, shredded

sweet chilli sauce, to serve

Method

STEP 1

Put the noodles in a pan of water and bring to the boil, simmer for 3 mins, then cool under running water. Drain thoroughly.

STEP 2

Cut the carrot into matchsticks using a knife or a mandoline. Cut the avocado into strips and the cucumber into thin sticks. Soak 2 of the rice paper wraps in cold water for 1-2 mins until floppy.

STEP 3

Lift 1 sheet of rice paper out of the water, shake gently, then lay it carefully on a board. Place 2 prawns in the centre, with a mint leaf between them. Add a strip of avocado, pile some noodles on top, then add a layer of carrot and cucumber.

Fold the bottom half of the rice paper over, then fold the sides in and tightly roll it up. Repeat using the second wrapper and soak 2 more to make 2 more rolls.

STEP 4

Make the rest of the rolls up using the remaining 4 wraps and the shredded chicken instead of prawns. Serve the rolls with the sweet chilli sauce for dipping.

Cheese & bacon scones

Ingredients

100g butter, plus extra for greasing

10 rashers streaky bacon

275g self-raising flour

½ tsp baking powder

150ml milk

50ml vegetable oil

1 egg

handful snipped chives

150g grated cheddar

Method

STEP 1

Heat oven to 200C/180C fan/gas 6 and grease a 12-hole muffin tin. In a frying pan over a medium heat, fry the bacon for 5 mins until golden. Let it cool, then chop into chunks and set aside

STEP 2

In a bowl, combine the flour, baking powder and 1 tsp sea salt. Using your fingers, mix the butter into the flour mixture until it resembles breadcrumbs

STEP 3

In a small bowl, whisk together the milk, oil and egg. Tip into the dry mixture, and gently mix until the flour mixture is mostly moistened (lumps will remain). Stir in the bacon, chives and cheese, then spoon the batter into the muffin tin.

STEP 4

Put the muffin tin in the oven and bake for 20 mins or until the tops are golden brown. Serve warm.

Gyoza

Ingredients

2 tbsp cornflour

26 ready-made gyoza skins, defrosted if frozen (see tip)

2-3 tbsp vegetable oil

For the filling

4 spring onions, ends trimmed, roughly chopped

2 large leaves of Savoy or pointed cabbages, hard stem removed, roughly chopped

a 1½cm piece of ginger, peeled and chopped

1 garlic clove

50g water chestnuts, about 5 (drained weight)

2 tsp soy sauce

2 tsp oyster sauce

1 tsp cooking saké

½ tsp sesame oil

140g minced pork or chicken

For the soy dipping sauce

2 tbsp soy sauce

1 tbsp rice vinegar

2 tsp sesame oil

For the yuzu dipping sauce

2 tbsp soy sauce

2 tbsp Yuzu juice

2 tsp peanut oil

Method

STEP 1

Put the spring onions, cabbage, ginger and garlic in a food processor, and whizz to a fine mix (or finely chop by hand).

STEP 2

Add the water chestnuts and pulse to chop, but not too finely – these will add a nice crunchy texture. Add the soy sauce, oyster sauce, sake, sesame oil and a pinch of salt, and whizz again.

STEP 3

Tip the **Ingredients** into a bowl and add the minced pork or chicken. Mix by hand until well combined. Chill until ready to use.

STEP 4

Have a pot of water to hand. Sprinkle the cornflour onto a plate. To assemble the gyoza, hold the dumpling skin in the palm of one hand and put a heaped teaspoon of the filling onto the centre of the skin.

STEP 5

Dip your finger in the water and wipe around the edge of the skin – this will moisten it and help the edges stick together.

STEP 6

Bring the edges of the skin together. Pinch pleats along one side, then press each pleat against the opposite flat side of the skin. With each pinch make sure that you are sealing the parcel and keeping the filling in the centre. Put each gyoza onto the plate dusted with cornflour. Can be covered with cling film and chilled for up to 8 hrs.

STEP 7

Cook the gyoza in batches. Heat a non-stick frying pan with 1 tbsp vegetable oil. Brush off any excess cornflour from the bases of the dumplings. Fry the gyoza on one side only – don't turn them over, you just want one crispy side. They should be golden brown after about 2 mins.

STEP 8

Add a good splash of water to the pan and cover with a steaming lid or a large sheet of foil with a few holes poked in the top. Cook over a medium heat for 3-5 mins until the water has evaporated and the gyoza filling is cooked through. Set aside while you cook the rest.

STEP 9

Mix all the dipping sauce **Ingredients** and serve alongside the dumplings in dipping bowls. You can serve with both or just one dipping sauce.

Chicken pakoras

Ingredients

700g boneless chicken, cut into bite-sized pieces

2 tbsp cornflour

50g rice flour

40g gram flour, sieved

3 dried chillies, crushed or 3 green chillies, finely chopped

½ tsp chilli powder

½ tsp curry powder

½ tsp ground coriander

½ tsp cumin

2 small onions, chopped

small bunch of coriander, finely chopped

vegetable oil, for deep-frying

sweet chilli sauce or green chutney, to serve

Method

STEP 1

Put the chicken in a large bowl, then use your hands to coat the pieces in the cornflour. Mix in the rice flour, followed by the gram flour. Add the chillies, spices, onion, coriander and 1 tsp salt. Mix well with your hands.

STEP 2

Gradually add around 150ml water until the **Ingredients** have become moist and ever-so-slightly wet. You may not need all the water (adding too much will stop the pakora mixture binding).

STEP 3

Fill a deep pan no more than a third full with vegetable oil and heat to 180C. Squeeze a small amount of the pakora mixture together before carefully lowering into the hot oil with a spoon. Fry for 8-10 mins, turning regularly, until cooked through and browned all over. Set aside on a plate lined with kitchen paper while you repeat with the remaining mixture, frying in small batches. Serve hot with a sweet chilli sauce or green chutney.

Warm chickpea salad

Ingredients

1 red onion, cut into wedges

2 courgettes, thickly sliced

1 red pepper, seeded and cut into large chunks

375g ripe tomato, halved

5 tbsp olive oil

juice of half lemon

3 tbsp chopped fresh mixed herbs (such as chives, parsley and mint) or 3 tbsp parsley

2 x 400g cans chickpeas, drained

100g feta cheese, cut into cubes

Method

STEP 1

Preheat the oven to fan 200C/ conventional 220C/gas 7. Put the onion, courgettes, pepper and tomatoes in a shallow roasting tin and season with black pepper. Drizzle with 2 tbsp of the olive oil and toss well. Roast for 30 minutes, stirring halfway through, until the vegetables are cooked and beginning to turn brown.

STEP 2

Meanwhile, mix the lemon juice and remaining olive oil to make a dressing. Season with salt and pepper and stir in the herbs.

STEP 3

When the vegetables are cooked, allow them to cool for 5 minutes, then tip into a bowl with the chickpeas, feta and dressing. Toss lightly before serving. Leftovers are delicious cold and served with pitta bread.

Fruity flapjack cookies

Ingredients

125g jumbo oats

150g softened butter

100g light muscovado sugar

1 egg

1 tbsp golden syrup

½ tsp vanilla extract

100g self-raising flour

100g mixed dried fruit or raisins

75g dried apricots, finely chopped

50g desiccated coconut

½ tsp ground cinnamon (optional)

Method

STEP 1

Heat the oven to 180C/160C fan/gas 4. Scatter the oats over a baking tray and bake for 20 mins, turning once until lightly browned. Remove from the oven and set aside to cool. Tip the butter and sugar into a bowl and beat with an electric whisk for 2 mins until fluffy. Crack in the egg and add the golden syrup and vanilla, then beat until completely combined. Scatter in the flour, all the dried fruit, the coconut, cinnamon (if using), the toasted oats and a pinch of salt. Beat again until everything is combined and you have a thick dough. Use the dough straightaway or cover and chill for up to two days.

STEP 2

Line two baking sheets with baking parchment and arrange six large spoonfuls of dough on each, well- spaced apart. Bake for 15 mins (or 18-20 mins if the dough is fridge-cold) until the cookies have spread and are brown at the edges but soft in the middle. Leave to cool on the baking sheet for 5 mins, then transfer to a wire rack and leave to cool completely. Will keep in an airtight container or tin for up to five days.

Bumper oat cookies

Ingredients

175g butter

175g demerara sugar

100g golden syrup

85g plain flour

½ tsp bicarbonate of soda

250g porridge oats

1 tsp ground cinnamon

100g each of ready-to-eat dried apricots, chopped and stem ginger, chopped

75-80g pack dried sour cherries

2 tbsp boiling water

1 medium egg, beaten

Method

STEP 1

Heat the oven to 180C/fan160C/gas 4. Line several baking sheets with baking parchment or non-stick sheets. Warm the butter, sugar and golden syrup in a large saucepan over a medium heat until the butter has melted. Stir in the flour, bicarbonate of soda, oats, cinnamon, dried fruits and ginger, then the water and finally the egg. Leave to cool until easy to handle.

STEP 2

With dampened hands, shape the mixture into 18 large balls, then flatten them onto the baking sheets – allowing plenty of space for spreading – and bake for 15-20 mins until golden. (This will give a soft, chewy cookie. For a crisper one, reduce the heat to 160C/fan140C/gas 3 and bake for a further 5-10 mins.)

STEP 3

Allow the cookies to cool on the trays briefly, then lift onto to a cooling rack. Will keep in an airtight container, separated with baking parchment, for up to 1 week.

Date & peanut butter dip

Ingredients

1 tbsp crunchy peanut butter (30g)

2 dates, finely chopped (10g)

120g bio yogurt

1-2 sticks celery, cut into shorter, thinner lengths

1 green pepper, deseeded and cut into strips

Method

STEP 1

Mash the peanut butter and dates together using a fork, then stir in the yogurt. Divide between two small bowls, or pots with lids for packing into lunchboxes. Will keep covered and chilled for up to three days. Serve with the vegetables for dipping.

Apple flapjacks

Ingredients

175g butter, plus extra for the tin

2-3 apples (about 350g), peeled, cored and chopped into small pieces

200g golden syrup

150g light brown soft sugar

300g porridge oats

50g dried apples, chopped

1/2 tsp ground cinnamon (optional)

Method

STEP 1

Heat the oven to 180C/160C fan/ gas 4. Butter the base of a 20 x 20cm square tin and line with baking parchment. Tip the chopped apples into a small saucepan with 2 tsp water and cook over a medium heat for 3-4 mins until the apples are just soft enough to crush, but there's still a little water left in the pan. If needed, add a little more water and cook the apples for slightly longer. Remove from the heat and crush the apples using a potato masher or a fork to break up slightly, then tip into a bowl and set aside.

STEP 2

Tip the butter, golden syrup and sugar into the pan and warm through over a low heat until the butter has melted and the sugar has dissolved. Remove from the heat and set aside.

STEP 3

Combine the oats, dried apple and cinnamon, if using, in a large bowl. Tip in the buttery syrup mix and cooked apples, then stir to combine. Tip the flapjack mixture into the prepared tin and press down firmly. Level the surface using a spatula, then bake for 25-30 mins until golden and bubbling at the sides. Leave to cool. Cut into 16 pieces. Will keep in an airtight container for three days.

Autumn piccalilli with pear

Ingredients

2 small cauliflower, cut into small florets

400g silverskin or pearl onion

600g courgette, cut into small chunks (about 2cm pieces)

6 firm pears, cored, and cut as the courgettes

100g salt

1.7l cider vinegar

finger-length piece fresh root ginger, grated

2 tbsp coriander seeds

3 tbsp brown or black mustard seeds

300g golden caster sugar

8 tbsp cornflour

5 tbsp English mustard powder

3 tsp turmeric

Method

STEP 1

In a bowl, mix together the vegetables, pears and salt with 2 litres of cold water, then cover and leave overnight.

STEP 2

The next day, drain the brine from the vegetables, rinse briefly, then tip into a large saucepan with the vinegar, ginger, coriander seeds, mustard seeds and sugar. Bring to the boil and simmer for 8-10 mins until the veg is just tender but still with a little bite. Drain the vegetables, reserving the liquid, and set aside while you make the sweet mustard sauce.

STEP 3

In a large bowl, stir together the cornflour, mustard powder and turmeric, then gradually pour in the hot vinegar while whisking, until you have a lump-free, thin yellow sauce. Return it to the saucepan and bubble over a low heat, stirring constantly, for 4 mins until smooth and thickened. Stir in the veg and spoon into five sterilised 500ml jars while hot, then seal. Once cool, enjoy straight away, or store in a cool, dark cupboard for 2-3 months. Refrigerate once opened.

SOUP AND STEW RECIPES FOR WEIGHT LOSS

Boxing Day soup

Ingredients

1 tbsp sunflower oil

1medium onion, chopped

2 celery sticks, chopped

2medium potatoes, about 350g/12oz total weight, peeled and cut into small chunks

1 tbsp curry paste

1.2l vegetable stock, made from a stock cube

550g leftover roasted or boiled vegetables, such as Brussels sprout, carrots, parsnips and squash, roughly chopped

natural yogurt or crème fraîche, to serve

Method

STEP 1

To fry the vegetables, heat the oil in a large saucepan and fry the onion for 5 minutes until golden. Stir in the celery and fry for 5 minutes, then tip in the potatoes and fry for a further 1-2 minutes, stirring often.

STEP 2

Stir in the curry paste, let it cook for a minute or so, then pour in the stock. Bring to the boil and stir well. Lower the heat, cover and simmer for 15-20 minutes until the potatoes are tender.

STEP 3

To serve, tip the leftover veg into the pan and warm through for a few minutes. Pour the soup into a food processor or blender and blitz to a smooth purée. Thin down to the consistency you like with hot water or stock (we added 300ml) then taste for seasoning. Cool and freeze, or serve in bowls with spoonfuls of yogurt or crème fraîche swirled on top.

Orange, carrot & mint soup

Ingredients

large knob of butter

700g carrot, peeled and thinly sliced

1 large onion, thinly sliced

1 large garlic clove, crushed

1l light vegetable stock

125ml freshly squeezed orange juice

2 tbsp finely chopped fresh mint

double cream, for drizzling - optional

Method

STEP 1

Melt the butter gently in a medium saucepan then add the carrots, onion and garlic. Cover with a lid and leave over a low heat, stirring occasionally, until the vegetables have softened but not coloured (about 12 minutes).

STEP 2

Pour in the stock and sprinkle in a little salt (if using a cube, hold back on the salt and adjust it at the end). Bring to the boil and simmer, partially covered, for 20-30 minutes or until the vegetables are very soft. Take off the heat and leave to cool for a few minutes.

STEP 3

Strain the vegetables through a sieve set over a bowl. Reserve the liquid. Transfer the vegetables to a food processor or blender. Process until smooth, adding enough of the strained liquid to make the mixture turn easily in the machine. Set the sieve over the cleaned pan and push the puréed vegetables through (this step is not essential but gives the soup a very smooth finish). Pour in the liquid and stir well to blend.

STEP 4

Tip in the orange juice and mint and gently reheat the soup. Stir and taste to see if more salt is needed, then pour into warmed bowls. If you like the idea of the cream, drizzle a little over the top.

Easy turkey soup

Ingredients

1 tbsp olive oil

1 large onion, halved and sliced into thin strips

1 red pepper, seeded and sliced into thin strips

2 tsp ground coriander

¼ - ½ tsp chilli flakes

3 tbsp basmati rice or long grain rice

1½ l hot turkey or chicken stock

250g/9oz turkey meat, cut into thin strips (leg meat will have the most flavour)

410g can chickpea, drained and rinsed

a handful of fresh coriander or flatleaf parsley, roughly chopped (optional)

Method

STEP 1

Heat the oil in a large pan, add the onion and fry for 5 minutes or so, stirring every now and then until it starts to soften.

STEP 2

To make the soup, add the red pepper, ground coriander, chilli and rice and stir round the pan for about a minute. Pour in the hot stock, stir in the turkey and chickpeas and season well. Bring to the boil, cover and simmer for 8-10 minutes, until the vegetables and rice are tender. Stir in the coriander or parsley and it's ready. (The soup may now be cooled and frozen for up to 1 month.)

Roast carrot soup with pancetta croutons

Ingredients

700g carrot, cut into batons

2 tbsp olive oil

4 garlic cloves, skin on

few thyme sprigs, plus extra to garnish

small knob of butter

2 onions, finely chopped

700ml chicken stock, made up with 1 cube

6 tbsp double cream

For the croutons

6 slices pancetta

2 thick slices rustic bread, cut into soldiers (we used sourdough)

drizzle olive oil

Method

STEP 1

Heat oven to 200C/180C fan/gas 6. Put the carrots, half the oil, the garlic and thyme in a roasting tin. Season and toss everything together. Pop in the oven and roast for 45-50 mins, or until tender and beginning to turn golden.

STEP 2

Meanwhile, heat the remaining oil and butter in a
large saucepan. Tip in the onions and cook over a
low heat for 10 mins until soft. When the carrots
are done, remove from the oven. Squeeze the soft
roasted garlic cloves out of their skins and pop in
the saucepan. Tip in the carrots and discard any
woody thyme stalks. Pour over the stock, bring to
the boil, then simmer for 10 mins.

STEP 3

To make the croutons, wrap the pancetta around
the soldiers, leaving the ends of the bread exposed.
Put on a baking tray, drizzle with a little oil and
grind over some black pepper. Bake for 10 mins

until the pancetta and bread edges are crisp. Drain on kitchen paper.

STEP 4

While the croutons are cooking, blitz the soup with a hand blender, then sieve into a clean saucepan, pressing to get as much liquid through as possible. Add 5 tbsp of the cream, heat through and season. Adjust the thickness with a little water, if you like. You can chill the soup for up to 1 day at this point, or freeze for 2 months. Reheat before serving. Serve drizzled with the remaining cream and garnished with thyme, with the croutons.

Mushroom soup

Ingredients

90g butter

2 medium onions, roughly chopped

1 garlic clove, crushed

500g mushrooms, finely chopped (chestnut or button mushrooms work well)

2 tbsp plain flour

1l hot chicken stock

1 bay leaf

4 tbsp single cream

small handful flat-leaf parsley, roughly chopped, to serve (optional)

Method

STEP 1

Heat the butter in a large saucepan and cook the onions and garlic until soft but not browned, about 8-10 mins.

STEP 2

Add the mushrooms and cook over a high heat for another 3 mins until softened. Sprinkle over the flour and stir to combine. Pour in the chicken stock, bring the mixture to the boil, then add the bay leaf and simmer for another 10 mins.

STEP 3

Remove and discard the bay leaf, then remove the mushroom mixture from the heat and blitz using a hand blender until smooth. Gently reheat the soup and stir through the cream (or, you could freeze the soup at this stage – simply stir through the cream when heating). Scatter over the parsley, if you like, and serve.

Smoked haddock chowder

Ingredients

450g smoked cod or smoked haddock (undyed)

1 bay leaf

2 tbsp light olive oil

50g butter

2 onions, finely chopped

2 leeks, halved lengthways and thinly sliced

3 celery sticks, thinly sliced

sweetcorn kernels from 1 corn-on-the-cob, or 140g/5oz frozen sweetcorn

900g potato, peeled and diced

3 garlic cloves, crushed with 1 tsp sea salt

2 tsp chopped fresh thyme or ½ tsp dried thyme

600ml milk

chopped fresh parsley, for sprinkling

Method

STEP 1

Put the fish in a deep frying pan with the bay leaf and 600ml/1 pint boiling water. Cover and simmer for 2 minutes. Turn off the heat and leave to stand, covered, for a further 5 minutes. Drain, reserving the liquid, then flake the fish.

STEP 2

Heat the oil and butter in a deep saucepan. Add the vegetables and garlic and fry over a high heat until starting to soften. Stir in the thyme and the reserved cooking liquid and bring to the boil. Reduce the heat and simmer for 10 minutes until the vegetables have softened.

STEP 3

Pour half the soup into a bowl and mash with a potato masher or fork. Return to the pan with the milk and fish. Simmer for 3 minutes, taste and season if needed. Sprinkle with chopped parsley to serve.

Nettle soup

Ingredients

1 tbsp olive oil, plus extra for drizzling

1 onion, chopped

1 carrot, diced

1 leek, washed and finely sliced

1 large floury potato (Maris Piper or similar), thinly sliced

1l vegetable stock

400g stinging or Dead nettles, washed, leaves picked (see tips below)

50g butter, diced

50ml double cream

Method

STEP 1

Heat the oil in a large saucepan over a medium heat. Add the onion, carrot, leek and potato, and cook for 10 mins until the vegetables start to soften.

Add the stock and cook for a further 10-15 mins until the potato is soft.

STEP 2

Add the nettle leaves, simmer for 1 min to wilt, then blend the soup. Season to taste, then stir in the butter and cream. Serve the soup drizzled with extra oil and scattered with dead nettle flowers, if you have them.

Pumpkin & bacon soup

Ingredients

1 tbsp vegetable oil

50g butter

1 onion, finely chopped

150g maple-cured bacon, cut into small pieces

½ Crown Prince pumpkin or onion squash, peeled, deseeded and cut into medium chunks (you need about 500g pumpkin flesh)

1l chicken stock

100ml double cream

3 tbsp pumpkin seeds, toasted

maple syrup, for drizzling

Method

STEP 1

In a large, heavy-bottomed pan, heat the oil with 25g butter. Add the onion and a pinch of salt and cook on a low heat for 10 mins or until soft. Add 60g bacon and cook for a further 5 mins until the bacon releases its fat. Then increase the heat to medium, add the pumpkin and stock and season. Bring to the boil, then reduce the heat to a simmer, cover with a lid and cook for about 40 mins until the pumpkin is soft. Pour in the cream, bring to the boil again and remove from the heat. Set aside some of the liquid, then blend the remaining pumpkin until smooth and velvety, adding liquid back into the pan bit by bit as you go (add more liquid if you like it thinner). Strain through a fine sieve, check the seasoning and set aside.

STEP 2

Melt the remaining butter in a pan over a high heat and fry the rest of the bacon with black pepper for 5 mins. Divide the bacon between four bowls, reheat the soup and pour over. To serve, sprinkle over the pumpkin seeds and drizzle with maple syrup.

Mum's leek & potato soup with mustard toasts

Ingredients

50g butter

8 rashers streaky bacon, chopped

5 large leeks, sliced

2 large potatoes, cubed

1.2l vegetable stock

2 bay leaves

300ml milk

handful chopped parsley

For the toasts

1 long thin baguette

4 tbsp olive oil

1 tbsp wholegrain mustard

Method

STEP 1

Melt the butter in a large pan, add the bacon and fry it until it is just starting to colour. Add the leeks and potatoes, then stir well until they are glistening.

STEP 2

Add the stock and bay leaves, season and bring to the boil. Partly cover and simmer for 15 mins, until everything is cooked. Fish out the bay leaves, then purée the soup in batches in a food processor or blender. Return to the pan and stir in the milk. Reheat gently and season to taste. Add more stock or water if the soup seems too thick (this will depend on the size of your potatoes). Sprinkle with parsley to serve.

STEP 3

Make the toasts: heat oven to 200C/fan 180C/gas 6. Cut the baguette into thin diagonal slices. Mix the oil and mustard together, then brush over both sides of the bread. Spread them on a large baking sheet and bake for 10 mins. Serve with the soup for dipping. They can be baked earlier in the day and served cold or warmed through in the oven.

Thai pumpkin soup

Ingredients

1.5kg pumpkin or squash, peeled and roughly chopped

4 tsp sunflower oil

1 onion, sliced

1 tbsp grated ginger

1 lemongrass, bashed a little

3-4 tbsp Thai red curry paste

400ml can coconut milk

850ml vegetable stock

lime juice and sugar, for seasoning

1 red chilli, sliced, to serve (optional)

Method

STEP 1

Heat oven to 200C/180C fan/gas 6. Toss the pumpkin or squash in a roasting tin with half the oil and seasoning, then roast for 30 mins until golden and tender.

STEP 2

Meanwhile, put the remaining oil in a pan with the onion, ginger and lemongrass. Gently cook for 8-10 mins until softened. Stir in the curry paste for 1 min, followed by the roasted pumpkin, all but 3 tbsp of the coconut milk and the stock. Bring to a simmer, cook for 5 mins, then fish out the lemongrass. Cool for a few mins, then whizz until smooth with a hand blender, or in a large blender in batches. Return to the pan to heat through, seasoning with salt, pepper, lime juice and sugar, if it needs it. Serve drizzled with the remaining coconut milk and scattered with chilli, if you like.

Quick tomato soup with cheesy garlic dippers

Ingredients

400g can cherry tomatoes

1 tbsp caster sugar

100ml vegetable stock

dash each Tabasco and Worcestershire sauce

2 tbsp mascarpone

few torn basil leaves (optional)

For the dippers

1 medium ciabatta roll, halved

1 garlic clove, halved

125g ball mozzarella cheese, shredded

Method

STEP 1

Put the tomatoes, sugar, stock and sauces into a medium pan with some salt and pepper. Bring to a simmer and cook for 5-10 mins. Stir in the mascarpone and blend to a smooth soup. Return to the pan and keep warm while you make the dippers.

STEP 2

Heat the grill to high and toast the ciabatta until golden. Rub with the garlic, season, then top with the cheese and grill until melted and golden. Slice into fingers and serve with the soup, sprinkled with the basil, if using.

Easy pea & mint soup

Ingredients

450g bag frozen peas

800ml hot water (straight from the kettle)

1 tbsp vegetable bouillon powder

small handful of chopped fresh mint, to serve

cream, to serve

Method

STEP 1

Tip the frozen peas into a blender and pour over the hot water from a kettle. Leave the peas to defrost, then reserve 1 tbsp peas. Add a handful mint and the vegetable bouillon powder to the rest. Blitz until smooth, then chill. Serve, drizzled with cream and scattered with some chopped mint and the reserved peas.

Red lentil & coconut soup

Ingredients

100g red lentils

1 heaped tsp turmeric

1 tbsp coarsely grated ginger

2 garlic cloves, sliced

1l vegetable stock

400ml can coconut milk

2 leeks, well washed and sliced

2 handfuls baby spinach (approx 50g/2oz)

Supercharged topping

2 limes, cut into wedge

Method

STEP 1

Tip the lentils into a large pan and add the turmeric, ginger and garlic. Pour in the stock, then cover the pan and simmer for 15 mins until the lentils have softened.

STEP 2

Pour in the coconut milk, stir in the leeks, cover and cook for 10 mins more.

STEP 3

Add the spinach and cook just to wilt it, then spoon into bowls and squeeze over the lime juice.

White velvet soup with smoky almonds

Ingredients

2 tsp rapeseed oil

2 large garlic cloves, sliced

2 leeks, trimmed so they're mostly white in colour, washed well, then sliced (about 240g)

200g cauliflower, chopped

2 tsp vegetable bouillon powder

400g cannellini beans, rinsed

fresh nutmeg, for grating

100ml whole milk

25g whole almonds, chopped

½ tsp smoked paprika

2 x 25g slices rye bread, to serve

Method

STEP 1

Heat the oil in a large pan. Add the garlic, leeks and cauliflower and cook for about 5 mins, stirring frequently, until starting to soften (but not colouring).

STEP 2

Stir in the vegetable bouillon and beans, pour in 600ml boiling water and add a few generous gratings of the nutmeg. Cover and leave to simmer for 15 mins until the leeks and cauliflower are tender. Add the milk and blitz with a hand blender until smooth and creamy.

STEP 3

Put the almonds in a dry pan and cook very gently for 1 min, or until toasted, then remove from the heat. Scatter the paprika over the almonds and mix well. Ladle the soup into bowls, top with the spicy nuts and serve with the rye bread.

Leek & butter bean soup with crispy kale & bacon

Ingredients

4 tsp olive oil

500g leeks, sliced

4 thyme sprigs, leaves picked

2 x 400g cans butter beans

500ml vegetable bouillon stock

2 tsp wholegrain mustard

½ small pack flat-leaf parsley

3 rashers streaky bacon

40g chopped kale, any tough stems removed

25g hazelnuts, roughly chopped

Method

STEP 1

Heat 1 tbsp oil in a large saucepan over a low heat. Add the leeks, thyme and seasoning. Cover and cook for 15 mins until softened, adding a splash of water if the leeks start to stick. Add the butter beans with the water from the cans, the stock and mustard. Bring to the boil and simmer for 3-4 mins until hot. Blend the soup in a food processor or with a stick blender, stir through the parsley and check the seasoning.

STEP 2

Put the bacon in a large, non-stick frying pan over a medium heat. Cook for 3-4 mins until crispy, then set side to cool. Add the remaining 1 tsp oil to the pan, and tip in the kale and hazelnuts. Cook for 2 mins, stirring until the kale is wilted and crisping at the edges and the hazelnuts are toasted. Cut the bacon into small pieces, then stir into the kale mixture.

STEP 3

Reheat the soup, adding a splash of water if it is too thick. Serve in bowls sprinkled with the bacon & kale mixture.

Cauliflower soup with chorizo and garlic croutons

Ingredients

2 tbsp olive oil

1 onion, chopped

1 cauliflower, cut into florets

2 garlic cloves, finely chopped

500ml chicken or vegetable stock

5cm long piece of chorizo, cut from a ring

1 large slice of crusty bread

2 tbsp double cream

small bunch parsley, chopped

Method

STEP 1

Heat 1 tbsp oil in a saucepan over a medium heat. Add the onion along with a pinch of salt. Cook until soft, about 6 mins, then tip in the cauliflower and half the garlic. Give everything a good stir, then pour in the stock. Cook for 12 mins or until the cauliflower is tender.

STEP 2

Meanwhile, peel the chorizo, then chop into small pieces. Toast the bread, then tear or cut into crouton-sized pieces. Heat the remaining oil in a frying pan, add the chorizo and fry until crisp. Tip in the bread and remaining garlic and cook for a minute or so until everything is nicely coated in the chorizo oils. Set aside.

STEP 3

Using a stick blender, blitz the soup with the double cream and season to taste. Reheat if necessary, then divide between two bowls. Mix the parsley with the chorizo and croutons, and top generously.

Smoked mackerel chowder with hedgehog garlic bread

Ingredients

4 garlic cloves, crushed

50g butter, plus a large knob for the chowder, softened

1 small round loaf of bread

1 tsp vegetable oil, for cooking

4 celery sticks, finely chopped, plus a few leaves to serve

1 onion, finely chopped

3 tbsp plain flour

600ml whole milk

2 large potatoes, cut into cubes

200g pack smoked peppered mackerel, flaked

200g frozen sweetcorn

Method

STEP 1

Heat oven to 220C/200C fan/gas 7. Mash the garlic with 50g butter. Slice the bread first one way, then the other (in a hedgehog pattern), but do not cut all the way through. Stuff the crevices with garlic butter, then wrap loosely in foil, leaving the top open to crisp, and bake for 20 mins while you make the chowder.

STEP 2

Heat a knob of butter in a saucepan with the oil. Tip in the celery and onion, cook for 5 mins or until soft, then add the flour and mix to a paste. Pour in the milk, a little at a time, and cook until smooth and the consistency of double cream. Add the potatoes and half the mackerel, cover and simmer for 15 mins until the potatoes are cooked.

STEP 3

Flake the remaining mackerel, add to the chowder with the sweetcorn and simmer for 1-2 mins until the sweetcorn is cooked. Splash in a little water if it is too thick. Ladle into bowls, scatter over the celery leaves and serve with the bread for dunking.

Fresh & light chowder

Ingredients

100g smoked haddock fillets and 100g unsmoked, skin on

500ml skimmed milk

500ml vegetable stock

2 thyme sprigs

1 tsp vegetable oil

1 onion, finely chopped

1 garlic clove, finely chopped

1 leek, sliced

1 large sweet potato, diced

200g can sweetcorn in water, drained

50g red lentils

small handful parsley, chopped

crusty bread, to serve

Method

STEP 1

Place the fish in a deep frying pan, then add the milk, stock and thyme. Bring to the boil and take off the heat; leave until cool enough to handle. Take out the fish (reserving the liquid), peel off the skin and flake the fish onto a plate, to use later.

STEP 2

Meanwhile, heat the oil in a large saucepan. Gently fry the onion, garlic and leek for 8-10 mins until soft and translucent. Add the sweet potato, sweetcorn and lentils, then pour over the liquid you cooked the fish in. Bring to the boil and simmer for 30 mins. Check the seasoning and semi-blitz with a hand blender – I like to leave it quite rough. Add the flaked fish and chopped parsley. Serve piping hot with some crusty bread.

Bouillabaisse

Ingredients

1 leek, green top left whole, white finely sliced

small bunch fresh thyme

3 bay leaves

bunch parsley, stalks whole, leaves roughly chopped

2 strips of orange peel

1 mild red chilli

4 tbsp olive oil

2 onions, chopped

1 leek

1 fennel, fronds picked and reserved, fennel chopped

4 garlic cloves, minced

1 tbsp tomato purée

1 star anise

2 tbsp Pernod, optional, if you have it

4 large, ripe tomatoes, chopped

large pinch (⅓ tsp) saffron strands

1 ½l fish stock

100g potato, one peeled piece

1kg of filleted mixed Mediterranean fish, each fillet cut into large chunks. (We used a mix of red and grey mullet, monkfish, John Dory and gurnard)

300g mussels, optional

For the rouille

2 garlic cloves

1 small chunk of red chilli (optional)

small pinch saffron

1 piece of potato, cooked in the broth, (see above)

1 egg yolk

100ml olive oil

1 tbsp lemon juice

For the croutons

½ baguette, thinly sliced

1 tbsp olive oil

Method

STEP 1

To make the croutons heat oven to 200C/180C fan/gas 6. Lay the slices of bread on a flat baking tray in a single layer, drizzle with olive oil and bake for 15 mins until golden and crisp. Set aside – can be made a day ahead and kept in an airtight container.

STEP 2

Use a layer of the green part of the leek to wrap around and make a herb bundle with the thyme, bay, parsley stalks, orange peel and chilli. Tie everything together with kitchen string and set aside.

STEP 3

Heat the oil in a very large casserole dish or stock pot and throw in the onion, sliced leek and fennel and cook for about 10 mins until softened. Stir through the garlic and cook for 2 mins more, then add the herb bundle, tomato purée, star anise, Pernod if using, chopped tomatoes and saffron. Simmer and stir for a minute or two then pour over the fish stock. Season with salt and pepper, bring to a simmer, then add the piece of potato. Bubble everything gently for 30 mins until you have a thin tomatoey soup. When that piece of potato is on the brink of collapse, fish it out and set aside to make the rouille.

STEP 4

While the broth is simmering make the rouille by crushing the garlic, chilli and saffron with a pinch of salt in a mortar with a pestle. Mash in the cooked potato to make a sticky paste then whisk in the egg yolk and, very gradually, the olive oil until you make a mayonnaise-like sauce. Stir in the lemon juice and set aside.

STEP 5

Once the chunky tomato broth has cooked you have two options: for a rustic bouillabaisse, simply poach your fish in it along with the mussels, if you're using (just until they open) and serve. For a refined version, remove the herb bundle and star anise. Using a handheld or table-top blender, blitz the soup until smooth. Pass the soup through a sieve into a large, clean pan and bring to a gentle simmer. Starting with the densest fish, add the chunks to the broth and cook for 1 min before adding the next type. With the fish we used, the order was: monkfish, John Dory, grey mullet, snapper. When all the fish is in, scatter over the mussels, if using, and simmer everything for about 5 mins until just cooked and the mussels have opened.

STEP 6

Use a slotted spoon to carefully scoop the fish and mussels out onto a warmed serving platter, moisten with just a little broth and scatter over the chopped parsley. Bring everything to the table. Some people eat it as two courses, serving the broth with croutons and rouille first, then the fish spooned into the same bowl. Others simply serve it as a fish stew. Whichever way you choose the rouille is there to be stirred into the broth to thicken and give it a kick.

Witches' brew (Pea & bacon chowder)

Ingredients

1 tbsp olive oil

onion, finely chopped

1 garlic clove, crushed

650g frozen petits pois

750ml vegetable stock

6 rashers streaky bacon

1 tbsp butter, optional

Method

STEP 1

Heat the oil in a saucepan. Add the onion and gently cook over a medium heat for 5-6 mins until softened but not coloured. Add the garlic and cook for a further min. Stir in three-quarters of the petit pois, then pour in the stock. Bring to the boil and simmer for 10-12 mins. Meanwhile, grill the bacon until crisp.

STEP 2

Allow to cool for a few mins, then carefully transfer to a food processor and whizz until smooth. You might need to do this in two batches, depending on the size of your processor.

STEP 3

Return the soup to the pan and add the remaining petit pois. Bring to the boil and simmer for 2 mins or until the whole peas are tender. Season to taste, then stir in the butter, if using. Break the bacon into pieces and scatter over bowls or mugs of soup. The soup can be made up to a day ahead; just grill the bacon on the day.

Green pesto minestrone

Ingredients

2 tbsp olive oil

1 large onion, finely chopped

2 celery sticks, finely chopped

1.4l vegetable stock

2 small lemons, zested and juiced

170g orzo

120g frozen peas

250g frozen spinach

50g pesto

garlic flatbreads, to serve (optional)

60g parmesan (or vegetarian alternative), grated

Method

STEP 1

Heat the oil in a large saucepan, add the onion, celery and a pinch of salt, and fry for 8 mins until soft. Add the stock with the zest and juice of the lemons, and season. Stir in the orzo and cook for 5 mins, then add the peas and spinach, and cook for a further 5 mins. Swirl though the pesto and season.

STEP 2

Heat the flatbreads, if using, following pack instructions. Ladle the soup generously into bowls and top with a handful of parmesan. Serve with the flatbread to dip.

PART IV: FINNALY!

The Long Term Outlook on The Mayo Clinic Diet

The "Live It" phase of the Mayo Clinic diet incorporates healthy diet and lifestyle changes you can maintain for life.

People often say they're 'on a diet' to lose weight. This often implies something rigid, focuses on what you can't eat, and that's a negative experience.

Therefore, it's not surprising that most people eventually go "off" their diets and soon regain any weight they may have lost.

The Mayo Clinic Diet, on the other hand, isn't an "on-again-off-again" diet. The diet is designed to be practical and enjoyable so you'll stick with it for the long haul.

Talk with your doctor before starting the Mayo Clinic diet or any other diet — your doctor or a registered dietitian can recommend the best eating plan for you, based on your health needs.

The Surprising Truth about Exercising For Weight Loss

Exercising has many benefits. Resistance training can help with weight loss by maintaining muscle mass and boosting metabolism. Cardio can also help but may make you hungrier, so try to eat mindfully.

If you're trying to lose weight, you may be wondering how much you should be exercising and what types of exercise you should be doing.

At its simplest, losing weight means burning more calories than you consume. So, it makes sense to include exercise in your routine, since it helps you burn more calories.

However, vigorous exercise can also help you work up an appetite. This may cause confusion about the role of exercise in weight loss and whether it can help.

So, what exactly is the purpose of exercise if you're trying to lose weight? This book takes a look at the evidence to help you find the answer and figure out what's best for you.

Cardio

This is one of the most popular types of exercise for weight loss is aerobic exercise, also known as cardio. Examples include:

- walking
- running
- cycling
- swimming

Aerobic exercise doesn't have a major effect on your muscle mass, at least not compared to lifting weights. However, it is very effective at burning calories.

A 10-month study examined how cardio without dieting affected 141 people with obesity or overweight. Participants were split into three groups and not told to reduce calorie intake.

Those who burned 400 calories per cardio session (5 times per week) lost 4.3% of their body weight, while those who burned 600 calories per session (also 5 times per week) lost a little more, at 5.7%. The control group, which didn't exercise, actually gained 0.5% of their body weight.

Strength Exercise

All physical activity can help you burn calories. However, resistance training — such as weight lifting — has benefits that go beyond that. Resistance training helps increase the strength, tone, and amount of muscle you have.

One study of 141 older adults with obesity examined the effects of cardio, resistance training, or both on body composition during a period of intentional weight loss.

This study found that those who did no exercise or cardio alone lost fat but also lost more muscle and bone mass than the groups that did resistance training.

So, resistance training appears to have a protective effect on both muscle and bone during periods of reduced calorie intake.

Higher amounts of muscle also increase your metabolism, helping you burn more calories around the clock — even at rest. This is because muscle is more metabolically active than fat, meaning it requires more energy.

This also helps prevent the drop in metabolism that can occur alongside weight loss. Because of this, doing some form of resistance training is a crucial addition to an effective long-term weight loss plan.

It makes it easier to keep the weight off, which is actually much harder than losing it in the first place.

High Intensity interval Training

High intensity interval training (HIIT) is a type of exercise characterized by short bursts of intense exercise followed by a brief rest before repeating this cycle. HIIT can be done with cardio or resistance training exercises and provides the benefits of both

Most HIIT workouts are only 10–20 minutes long, but they offer some powerful benefits in regard to weight loss.

One 2017 review of 13 high quality studies found that HIIT and cardio exercise provided similar benefits — namely, reduced body fat and waist circumference — for people with overweight and obesity.

However, HIIT exercise achieved these same benefits with a 40% time savings compared to cardio. Because of the intensity of HIIT, you should consult a healthcare professional before starting a new HIIT routine, especially if you have known heart concerns.

Exercise and Appetitie

You've probably heard that physical exertion is a good way to work up an appetite, or maybe you even found yourself eating more than usual after a vigorous workout.

However, most research points to exercise having an appetite suppression effect. One study in 20 active, healthy adults noted that they ate more food in the meal prior to a workout than after — and actually found that, overall, participants ate less food on the days they exercised than the days they didn't

In another study in 26 women with obesity on low calorie diets, researchers found that short HIIT sessions had a strong appetite suppressing effect. Researchers have also noted that morning exercise appears to be more beneficial for energy balance and calorie intake than evening exercise — further supporting the theory that exercise can reduce appetite.

Regardless, more research is needed, and hunger responses to exercise are likely highly individual. If you're trying to lose weight but tend to eat more than usual after vigorous or long exercise sessions, consider shorter durations (like HIIT) or less intense exercise.